THROUGH
THE EYES
OF HOPE

THROUGH
THE EYES
OF HOPE

LACEY BUCHANAN
with BETHANY JETT

CHARISMA
HOUSE

Most CHARISMA HOUSE BOOK GROUP products are available at special quantity discounts for bulk purchase for sales promotions, premiums, fund-raising, and educational needs. For details, write Charisma House Book Group, 600 Rinehart Road, Lake Mary, Florida 32746, or telephone (407) 333-0600.

THROUGH THE EYES OF HOPE by Lacey Buchanan with Bethany Jett
Published by Charisma House
Charisma Media/Charisma House Book Group
600 Rinehart Road
Lake Mary, Florida 32746
www.charismahouse.com

Scripture quotations marked MEV are taken from the Modern English Version. Copyright © 2014 by Military Bible Association. Used by permission. All rights reserved.

Scripture quotations marked NIV are taken from the Holy Bible, New International Version˚, NIV˚. Copyright © 1973, 1978, 1984, 2011 by Biblica, Inc.˝ Used by permission of Zondervan. All rights reserved worldwide. www.zondervan.com. The "NIV" and "New International Version" are trademarks registered in the United States Patent and Trademark Office by Biblica, Inc.˝

Cover design by Justin Evans

Visit the author's website at http://christianbuchanan.blogspot.com.

Library of Congress Cataloging-in-Publication Data:

Names: Buchanan, Lacey, author.
Title: Through the eyes of hope / Lacey Buchanan with Bethany Jett.
Description: First edition. | Lake Mary : Charisma House, 2017. |
Includes
    bibliographical references.
Identifiers: LCCN 2016045413| ISBN 9781629991078 (hardback) |
ISBN
    9781629991085 (ebook)
Subjects: LCSH: Parents of children with disabilities--Religious life.
Classification: LCC BV4596.P35 B83 2017 | DDC 248.8/6--dc23
LC record available at https://lccn.loc.gov/2016045413

17 18 19 20 21 — 987654321
Printed in the United States of America

This book is dedicated to every parent of a child with special needs who has ever felt burned out, run-down, stretched too thin, overwhelmed, or ill-equipped.

God has called you, and He will equip you. Your circumstances don't define you, nor do they define the God we serve. His truths are still truth, and He will make good on His promises.

You. Are. Enough.

CONTENTS

ACKNOWLEDGMENTS

*I will lead the blind by ways they have not known, along
unfamiliar paths I will guide them; I will turn the darkness
into light before them and make the rough places smooth.
These are the things I will do; I will not forsake them.*
—ISAIAH 42:16, NIV

FIRST I WANT to thank God for leading me down the unfamiliar paths in my life, for turning my darkness into light, and for always being near. You held me close in my hardest moments and opened my blinded eyes to the overwhelming love that is who You are.

I have to say thank you to everyone who has supported my family over the last six years. Large and small gestures of kindness have come at just the right times and have carried me so many miles further than I could have ever gone alone.

Thank you to everyone who has followed us on social media for the last five years. Without all of you none of this would be possible. Thank you for loving my boy as if he were your own and opening your hearts and homes to us.

While mentioning everyone would fill a book of its own, I hold each one of you close to my heart. Many thanks to Marisa Graham, Cassandra Turner, Pamela Randolph, Amanda Parks, Shawna Ervin, Tabitha Copeland, Julie Dirks, Sara Castro, Dr. Roberto Flores, the staff at Riley Children's Hospital, *The Doctors* staff and crew, Special Kids Therapy and Nursing center and all their amazing therapists and staff, everyone at Tennessee School for the Blind, Joan and Dana McKenzie, Angie Lewis, Kelly Culbreth, Julie Thomas, Derrick Hartley, David and Tracy Higgins and family, the Follet family, Glenda Morrison, Sue and Ole Man Snyder, Hope Alford, Ashlyn Allen, Gina Yavelak, Sara Feinstein (for the amazing cover photo), all of Harvest View Church, and so many others whom I'm sure I am forgetting. Your kindness over the last six years has been what has gotten me through. None of you will ever truly know how the love you've shown me is forever etched on my heart. I will never be able to repay your kindness in a million lifetimes.

Thank you also to everyone at Charisma House for taking a chance on me. You have literally helped me to make a lifelong dream come true with this book, and your patience and willingness to guide me through this new-to-me territory is so appreciated!

To my agent, Amanda Luedeke, thank you for your guidance through this process and how you have believed in this project from the beginning.

Bethany Jett, my writer, who helped make this story come to life, thank you for your listening ear, your understanding when I needed a moment to cry, for laughing with me when I got to share the joys, and for crying with me when I shared the hardships. This has been therapeutic for me. Watching this book come to life has been an amazing experience, and I can't say thank you enough for making it happen!

To my parents, Wayne and Kathy Taylor, thank you for the steadfast love you have always shown me. In the ups and the downs I have always had one constant, and that was your love. It has carried me and held me so many times and in so many ways. The love a parent gives a child is truly invaluable, and I hit the lottery when I got you for parents.

To Chris, thank you for giving me the most precious gift I have ever received, our sweet boys. Our teenage dreams may not have turned out how we planned, but our boys have been more than I could have ever hoped for. Thank you for the good times that made me laugh and the hard times that made me grow.

Finally, to my boys, Christian and Chandler. I don't think any words could truly ever describe my love for you. No matter how hard I try, I have never been able to fully speak what my heart feels for you.

Christian, your bravery and joy for life has given me the courage to face my hardest days. I promised that you would never face a hard day alone, and I knew that if you could do it, so could I. You are amazing in every sense of the word.

Chandler, your laughter and love for life have given me a hope and purpose that I never had before. I didn't know I could love a mischievous little laugh as much as I love yours. You came to me right when I needed you most, and you have given my life so much joy.

To both of you, you two are world-changers. Don't ever forget it. And you are madly loved. You always have been and you always will be.

INTRODUCTION

The chains of love are stronger than the chains of fear.
—WILLIAM GURNALL, *THE CHRISTIAN*
IN COMPLETE ARMOUR

HERE HE COMES... Happy birthday to Christian!"
The blue draping blocked my view, but amid the newborn wails a stillness blanketed the operating room. My
husband, Chris, squeezed my hand before rushing over to the
bundle of nurses surrounding our son to see the extent of the
birth defect previously revealed by the ultrasounds.

The noise jumped to an alarming level as fifteen people's voices
overlapped in a jumble of questions.

As one set of doctors worked on Christian, another group
stitched my abdomen. The pulling and tugging sent waves of
nausea through me. Half-paralyzed and bound to the table, I
craned my neck as far as I could to get a glimpse of the furious
activity on the other side of the room.

"Is he OK?" I asked. The anesthesiologist seated behind me
responded by patting my shoulder.

Chris turned, red-eyed and pale. He came back and grabbed my hand again.

The flurry around Christian slowed as we stared at each other—the noise blurred into the background. I was inside my head yet outside of my body at the same time, swimming against a slow tide of seconds ticking by. Dust particles floated between us. I could have plucked one out of the thickened atmosphere if I'd wanted.

"Tell me it's not bad," I whispered, as a hot tear escaped down the slope of my cheek.

Chris withdrew into himself momentarily, finding the bearings he needed to say two small devastating words.

"It's worse."

What is life but God's daring invitation to a remarkable journey?[1]

Some people say Chris and I were faced with a crossroads that day, but the only path I've ever set my eyes upon is the one that leads to life. It isn't easy to pour out one's soul, to let others see the emotions shaped from difficult circumstances. This is a vulnerable practice. But I want to welcome you into our home, to invite you to listen behind closed doors and travel with us firsthand as we faced the most unexpected, trying, amazing adventure of our lives.

My prayer is that the lessons God taught us weren't learned in vain—that as you read our story, you'll find a renewed strength to face the trials that come your way, and that you'll learn to love more, worry less, and see God in the midst of adversity.

Chapter One

WHEN LIFE TAKES A TURN

We are all faced with a series of great opportunities
brilliantly disguised as impossible situations.
—CHARLES SWINDOLL

LESS THAN A month after applying to law school, I waved the coveted acceptance letter over my head. Chris scooped me up in his strong arms and together we danced a happy tango across the carpet Could life be more perfect?

The anticipation of fulfilling my childhood dream of becoming a lawyer left me energized, ready to take on the world. Excitement sweetened every moment.

Until two days later.

I came home from work, plopped on the couch, and realized the cramps I'd ignored all day hadn't gone away. In fact, they'd worsened. About an hour later the cramps intensified to the point where I couldn't get comfortable. No amount of cushion or repositioning provided relief. I felt a strange sensation and raced to the bathroom.

My period wasn't due for another two weeks, but when I saw the spotting, I knew something was off. I grabbed my phone to call my doctor but hesitated.

She's going to ask if I'm pregnant.

On a whim I shuffled through a toiletry bag and found a pregnancy test. Thank God for two-packs.

After I took the test, I set it on the vanity countertop.

Two pink lines.

Oh. My. Mercy.

I called Chris immediately. He wouldn't be home for another few hours, but there was no way I could keep this amazing news a secret.

We chatted excitedly and celebrated over the phone for several minutes before we said good-bye. No sooner had I hung up than the bleeding started again, horrifyingly red and thick. I buried my head in my hands.

No…no…God, no. Please.

Pain shot through my abdomen, and I thought I'd never make it out of the bathroom. I called my obstetrician, who squeezed me in for her earliest appointment the next day.

As soon as Chris walked in the door, tears streamed down my face as I waved the pregnancy stick in the air. He hugged me gently and rested his hand on my flat belly.

"Everything will be fine," I said, but inside I was dying. Each trip to the bathroom compounded my fears.

I barely slept that night.

The next morning I was ready to leave the house well before the proper time. At seven o'clock I couldn't wait any longer. As I drove, I thought of all the people around me, headed home or to their jobs, blissfully happy while my life felt like it was about to come crashing down.

God, please don't let me lose this baby. Save my baby.

ULTRASOUND #1

The outline of my uterus was the only distinguishable area as the technician moved the probe across my stomach, the black-and-gray void unchanging on the screen. We waited as she switched to a more invasive and uncomfortable process. The wand pressed inside me as she searched for evidence of life.

"It's too early for there to be a heartbeat," she told us. "Don't worry if we don't hear anything." With a few clicks of the computer mouse she snapped a few pictures then froze the screen and typed notes across a tiny round area.

The yolk sac.

The absence of a heartbeat was terrifying. I'd heard that miscarriage is "nature's way" of ending an abnormal pregnancy, that many women who experience a heavier-than-normal period may actually have miscarried without ever realizing it. But I *knew* I was pregnant, and I desperately wanted this baby, yet I felt powerless to protect the child inside me.

Why would God bless us with a life only to take it away?

When the exam was over, a grave-looking doctor came in to explain our situation. As he spoke, my mind latched onto only the most horrific words: "...progesterone...early...possible miscarriage. Nothing to do but wait."

"There has to be something we can do," Chris said.

"Yes," I looked at him. "We pray."

Why would God bless us with a life only to take it away?

Ultrasound #2

Three weeks later I balanced myself on the narrow table. I glanced at the doctor who'd joined us and squeezed my hands into fists as I waited for proof of life. The entire reason for this ultrasound was to determine if I had miscarried or if my baby had won the fight. At six weeks' gestation the heartbeat should be loud and strong, a good sign that the baby would hold on for the rest of the pregnancy.

The technician gently began the exam.

It was the moment of truth, and I was terrified.

Immediately the most beautiful steady *thump-thump, thump-thump* like thundering hooves echoed in the room. I closed my eyes, hands clasped over my heart in silent thanks to God.

For a few silent moments I memorized every rhythmic pulse and beat. My baby—our baby—still lived.

A week later, on my first night of law school, I sat in the hard-backed chair, laptop open, ready for note-taking. The experience became one of those "core memories," like from the kids' movie *Inside Out* where the cute emotions characters control the humans' brains. A brand-new path lay before me. As I sat waiting for the professor to begin his lecture, I wondered about my baby's future. The timing felt significant. He was coming to law school with me—maybe he'd be a lawyer![1]

The days passed in sweet routine. As my belly swelled, Chris and I narrowed down a list of names and started decorating the nursery. The Buchanan home was filled with young love and bright dreams for our family.

Halfway through the pregnancy we returned to the obstetrician's office for the standard anatomy ultrasound. I was showing enough to wear maternity clothes and already felt the baby's kicks and stretches.

Just for fun I'd taken a "gender prediction test" from Rite-Aid. Ecstatic to find out if our active baby was, in fact, male, Chris and I crossed our fingers in anticipation as the tech searched for the telltale body parts. Thankfully our little guy wasn't shy.

We looked at each other and smiled.

"Christian."

"Jinx," we said in unison, playing the childhood game.

As we watched his activity on the monitors, our technician asked a series of questions. Mesmerized by every kick and arm movement, we answered as best we could while we fell even more in love with our little boy. When the exam was over, we left the office hand in hand, completely unaware that our blue skies were about to turn gray.

Lacey Buchanan
December 26, 2010

Seriously having trouble breathing thanks to some tiny hands/elbows pressing into my lungs. Wouldn't have it any other way.

A GOD WINK

The next evening I turned on *60 Minutes* while I waited for Chris to get home. The episode was of a father who pushed his disabled son in races and marathons. Despite uneven terrain and long miles, they crossed the finish line together so that his son could experience life to the best of his ability.

We didn't have any idea at that point that something was wrong with Christian, but those pregnancy hormones had me boo-hooing until my nose hurt from blowing it so often.

I grabbed a piece of paper and penned a note to my unborn baby. It said in part:

You are my child and if something is wrong with you, nothing will change how much I love you.

Truer words were never spoken.

This is a God wink, when He inspires you to do something that foretells an event of epic proportion. We see this in the small things, and many times we don't know how God is using these small instances to work out a greater thing. His ways are mysterious. Some dismiss this as coincidence, but I believe the Holy Spirit prods and guides us.

God uses small instances to work out greater things.

Just as I felt compelled to write a note to Christian, God again nudged me. While I was cleaning the house that weekend, a strange sensation fell over me—a compulsion, really, to check our home voice mail.

Chris and I rarely used that phone, relying on our cells, but I couldn't shake the feeling. Plus, it allowed me to take a break from dusting, so I grabbed the receiver and punched in our code.

You have three unheard messages.

My body stiffened when I recognized my obstetrician's voice asking me to return her call right away.

Beep.

The second message began. Again the doctor urgently requested a return call.

Beep.

The final message. "Hi, Lacey. I've left a couple of messages regarding your ultrasound. It's *imperative* that you call me back *as soon as you can.*"

The blood in my veins chilled; the duster I'd been holding tumbled out of my hand.

I immediately called back the number she'd left, only to be greeted with a friendly automated message. "The offices are currently closed. If this is a medical emergency, please hang up and dial 9-1-1."

Thus began the longest weekend of my life.

I don't remember how we passed the time, but this marked the beginning of what would be extensive bouts of patience building. Someone joked to never pray for patience because God has a habit of teaching it to you instead of simply *gifting* that particular attribute.

It's amazing how life flips in an instant—how all is perfect, right, and peaceful until one call changes everything. We felt like we were in a television soap opera trapped in the middle of a long commercial break.

As we counted down the hours until the doctor's office reopened, we held fast to the promises of Scripture, specifically that God knows us as He forms us. (See Psalm 139.) While we didn't know what was wrong, we knew that God knew, and we saw God in every aspect of the created life inside me.

We thought about the passages of Scripture reminding us not to worry, but how does someone *not* worry when she has missed three phone calls from a doctor after a supposedly routine appointment?

Christian was an active baby, constantly tumbling around like a gymnast, so we prayed that there wasn't anything "too wrong." But the sound of desperation in the doctor's last message left me with an unshakable feeling that the news would be devastating.

Belly Book Entry: October 3, 2010

Got a call from your doctor about your ultrasound pictures. I'm not sure what's wrong, but I am sure God's going to take care of you.

ULTRASOUND #3

Our new technician, Jennifer, squirted the tepid blue gel on my belly, and we stared at the monitor with bated breath. Christian's form appeared, and his heartbeat was music to our ears. He kicked a foot, and we smiled.

Jennifer moved the transducer, focusing on Christian's face. While it was hard for us to distinguish the features hiding in the gray-and-black shadows, her trained eyes specifically targeted one area. When she inhaled sharply, a cold chill washed over me and I shivered.

Jennifer continued to take pictures and measure different areas of our baby's face. After a stretch of forever she wiped my belly with a soft cloth, helped me sit up, then turned on the lights. "I have to show this to the perinatologist. He'll read the ultrasound. We may be taking more pictures. Just hold tight."

With a sweet smile she walked out, gently shutting the door behind her.

Chris and I waited in silence, unable to name our fears.

Moments later Dr. Michael DeRoche followed Jennifer back into the room, performed the niceties, then stood next to the monitors, pointing out various areas of Christian's ultrasound.

He spoke gently and slowly, allowing us to comprehend the weight of his words. "It appears that we're looking at bilateral cleft lip and palate. You can see the darker area here," he said, pointing at one of the images. "This is the nose and top lip region, which appears to not be forming correctly."

Dr. DeRoche is an incredibly compassionate man. He always made us feel as if Christian was the most important baby on his roster. Never once did he mention abortion; he knew we loved our baby madly.

I lay back down, and Jennifer prepped my belly again so the doctor could get a firsthand look. He skillfully and tactfully guided the ultrasound images to show clearly the front and left side of Christian's face. We poked and prodded my stomach to try to make him turn, but Christian stubbornly kept the right side of his face hidden.

After about twenty minutes the doctor turned off the monitor. "This is an unusual and severe case. We'll be monitoring him closely."

Lacey Buchanan
October 11, 2010

Cannot see where God is going with all these things, but I'm keeping my trust in Him and praying He shows me soon.

Mounting Concerns

I prayed daily for the health of my little boy. We told our family about the bilateral cleft lip, and they cried with us, saddened about the surgeries he would have at such a young age.

Concern for Christian's situation grew with each ultrasound visit. These were scheduled every two weeks so that as Christian grew, we'd be able to see more of his features and formulate a plan. Each time I'd lay on the exam table as the team tried to get the whole picture. Oftentimes the news was worse than expected as they pieced together a new part of the puzzle, but the end result was always the same.

"Secondary to fetal position, we could not see the face clearly. Let's look again in two weeks."

The worry of the unknown haunted my thinking. There's a reason people say not to look up stuff on the Internet—a simple sneeze can turn into walking pneumonia after a few clicks online.

Waiting for answers is hard.

Despite the discouraging updates, the support we received was incredible. I wasn't actively sharing our story on social media, yet a kind stranger mailed a card that said she was praying for Christian. I often reminded myself that no matter what happened, there had been numerous others who have experienced much worse. Somehow if others' misfortunes were greater and they'd lived to tell the tale, I could be strong too.

We have friends and family members who have experienced great loss—deaths of relatives, cancer, hospice, tragic car fatalities, miscarriages, job losses. There are often no explanations for the *whys* and sometimes not even the *hows*.

It's easier to handle a situation when there is someone to blame. In the absence of a villain many people throw God into the defendant's seat, setting themselves up as judge and jury. Though tempted, I refused to let those thoughts take root. This can cause one to wander down dark trails of bitterness, and we were too early in this process to get lost in despair.

Instead we filled our days with the hope of holding our sweet baby. I longed to gaze into his eyes and tell him how much we loved him. That hope motivated us to keep going, so we stayed busy doing things we could control. Exercise. Work. Sleep. And ultrasounds every other week for the next five months.

All we could do when we found ourselves locked inside a tailspin of worry was choose hope and trust God.

Lacey Buchanan
February 10, 2011

Was just thinking about Christian. I wonder what color his eyes are. I can't wait to find out!!! I am so in love with this little boy!!!

ULTRASOUND SCARE

Christian's airway became a concern for our doctor, so at one of our ultrasounds during my third trimester a nurse informed me that it was time to schedule a cesarean. My mother's horrific story of her C-section sprinted into my mind. The anesthesiologist had injected the spinal block too high, leaving her struggling for breath on the operating table.

I couldn't help bursting into tears, startling the nurse, who was unaware of my memory flood flash. In a career where C-sections have become common place, she paused and smiled at me with sweet concern. "You're really worried about this, aren't you?"

I was.

Even to this day anesthesia is the worst part for me during Christian's surgeries, and I'm not even the one going under the knife. A C-section was necessary though. Not only was Christian breech, the C-section would allow the doctors time to deliver while leaving the umbilical cord in place to keep the oxygen flowing from my body to his while they checked and cleared his airway if needed. Those few seconds between when the cord is cut and the baby's first breath are precious and critical.

KNIT TOGETHER

God gave us a gift in Jennifer. Her son was born with a cleft palate too, and during each exam she was comforting. "He's going to be fine," she reassured me. "I've been through this, and it's going to be OK." She was our tech for many of our ultrasounds, and we loved her so much that we returned to her for our next baby's appointments.

During an ultrasound in early November I assumed my position on the table. Jennifer and I exchanged pleasantries and caught up a little before we fell into a comfortable silence. She was cruising along with her work, then suddenly gasped, "Wait—wait—wait—wait."

Alarmed, my senses went on high alert. "What's going on?"

"Baby's OK," she said as she ran out of the room. "Just wait."

I could hear Christian's heartbeat, and his little foot kicked every few seconds. I searched the fuzzy grays and blacks on the screen to see what she'd noticed, but I couldn't distinguish anything besides his head, round body, and little legs.

A few moments later Jennifer and the doctor rushed into the room and huddled over the machine. They determined the trespassing dark shape was an amniotic sheet. Although that news was scary, it was better than it being an amniotic band. The basic difference is that a sheet is connected at both ends to the placenta; bands are connected at only one end, while the other end free-floats. Thus there is a risk that the bands can attach to the baby, cut off the blood flow, and even cause the loss of a body part.

Unfortunately what we couldn't see were the two amniotic bands that had snaked themselves to the right side of Christian's face, pinning him to the placenta.

Even through these scary times, God reassured me of His love for me and Christian. He placed on my heart the Bible verses Psalm 139:13–14, which say, "For you created my inmost being; you knit me together in my mother's womb. I praise you because I am fearfully and wonderfully made" (NIV). I couldn't stop thinking about those words.

How could those words be true when we knew there was something wrong with Christian? I don't blame God for Christian's disability; I believe that God can *and has* used Christian's life already to bring joy and glory to Him. But honestly my heart took a slow, methodical journey to understand this truth, and God kept reminding me that Christian was fearfully and wonderfully made.

Christian is fearfully and wonderfully made. I, in my sin and craziness, am fearfully and wonderfully made. And this perspective helps me during encounters with others. No matter how people act, they also are fearfully and wonderfully made.

UNWAVERING LOVE

The world felt chaotic, but my love for Christian remained constant. It was the realization that God loves us this way—unchanging and unwavering—that helped me face each new morning.

Our days were full. I worked my shift at the day care and drove to law school two evenings each week. Chris and I were doing well, holding on to each other as couples do when there is uncertainty that affects them both.

In the evenings after work I'd lay on the couch and watch Christian's nightly choreography. I hadn't gained much weight with him, so each movement—every hiccup even!—caused a ripple against my ever-tightening skin. If Chris was home, I'd yell for him to come see.

Without fail the second Chris placed his hands on my belly, the kicks would stop. I don't think Chris felt him give one good kick during my pregnancy. It became a lighthearted joke that Christian was going to cause Daddy mischief.

In this way we enjoyed our second year of marriage, but it wasn't without a few bumps. Chris lost his job when I was six weeks along. The weight of Christian's early diagnosis dented our resolve, but we mustered the courage and faith to keep going.

The last half of my pregnancy felt like bad news after bad news, so my mother decided to throw me a fabulous baby shower. It was such a happy day full of friends, food, and gifts. We knew with the bilateral cleft that Christian wouldn't be able to take a bottle or pacifier, so it was slightly awkward to say, "Please don't buy those!"

We decorated in blues and browns with a custom-made two-tiered cake that was a replica of a cake design I'd found on Facebook. My aunt Joan decided that with all the heaviness surrounding the pregnancy, I needed something a little extra special. She joked that she scoured the entire southeastern United States to find the perfect cake. Her willingness to go above and beyond reminded me that God shows His love through people's kindness.

A beautiful fruit tray served as the centerpiece amongst appetizers and hors d'oeuvres on the kitchen island. Presents for Christian were piled high in the living room, and it felt like a perfectly typical baby shower celebration.

I wore my pretty navy blue sweater dress with white and gray stripes around the bottom, the same dress I wore to my college graduation. From the side it looked like I had stuffed a volleyball under my dress.

Though we had a lovely time, Christian's birth defect was the elephant in the room. Everyone knew—I wasn't shy about it—but no one wanted to talk about the issues we were facing. I resolved if I was ever a guest in a similar situation I would at least ask a simple, "How are you feeling?"

It takes a lot of courage to ask questions. No one wants to put a damper on a celebration, but it offers the chance to vent a little, to release what gets bottled up inside.

After nibbling sandwiches and drinking festive punch, it was time to cut the cake. I posed with the knife like a serial killer, ready to stab through the layers of vanilla and cream because of the pregnancy hormones. It was funny, but the real joke was a secret: my pregnancy was the easiest of any pregnancy stories I've ever heard—no morning sickness, nonexistent mood swings. Another God wink.

SMALL WIN

We had such an incredible time at the baby shower, and there were always people letting me know that they were praying for us. I treasured the kind words and held tight to God's promise that He works things out for the good of those who love Him (Rom. 8:28).

One event I was super excited to attend was the annual fair in Bell Buckle, a nearby town even smaller than ours. The day was gorgeously bright and clear. My mom and I perused the vendors' tents and carts, nonchalantly strolling through the exhibits. While it looked like a casual outing, I was on a mad hunt for a diaper bag. I didn't know exactly what I wanted, but I knew I would know it when I saw it—kinda like when you put on *the* wedding dress.

We'd walked around for a while before I had a "this is *the* bag" moment. The soft quilted blue bag with brown handles covered in polka dots was nestled between other handcrafted totes and purses. The sellers stitched Christian's name with their monogram machine while we waited. It became another small symbol of normalcy.

I'll never take for granted these little blessings, small reminders that God did care about the things I cared about, that despite the fact that my baby was having some difficulties inside me, he was perfectly loved and desperately wanted.

LABOR OF LOVE

However, we did have a couple more scares. One ultrasound showed that Christian had a club foot. It had grown out of shape because he wasn't able to move it properly. The problems seemed to pile on top of each other, and I feared anything else would cause an avalanche.

Then nine days before our scheduled C-section I started bleeding.

An ice storm raged outside, but we couldn't risk waiting it out. Chris led me to the car, then drove as fast as he could—a whopping ten miles per hour—through the terrible road conditions to the closest emergency room.

When we walked into the hospital, a nurse behind the counter gave me a once-over. "Can I help you?"

The words flooded from my mouth. "I'm thirty-seven weeks pregnant, my baby has a birth defect, and I think I'm in labor."

Her eyes rounded. She grabbed a wheelchair right away and ran me all the way to the ER. Chris couldn't keep up with her. By the time he got to my room, I'd slipped into a gown with the exam bed covers tucked around me.

The doctors performed an exam, but although I was one centimeter dilated, I wasn't in active labor. We returned home with a new restriction upon us. No more "date nights" for now.

We were relieved but still anxious, having no real idea what was ahead of us. Through those first nine months God taught us that when life takes a dramatic turn, He is unchanging, even in our poorest circumstance or worst nightmare.

Chapter Two

TRUSTING GOD WHEN THINGS GO WRONG

God doesn't call us to be comfortable. He calls us to trust Him so completely that we are unafraid to put ourselves in situations where we will be in trouble if He doesn't come through.
—FRANCIS CHAN, *CRAZY LOVE*

CHRISTIAN'S WAILS TUGGED at my heart, but I wasn't able to hold him, comfort him. My baby needed me, but he needed us to figure out what was wrong even more. Our plastic surgeon removed the amniotic bands from Christian's face while my own doctors stitched me up. Just before Christian was whisked away for his Apgar testing, a different doctor popped him above the C-section curtain.

I saw a blur of dark hair before he disappeared.

Within minutes Christian was rushed away from the operating room to the neonatal intensive care unit (NICU) for monitoring and evaluation, and I was taken to the recovery area. We were left with zero answers and no baby to cuddle.

I wanted to feel his skin as he lay on my chest, his heart beating in rhythm with my own. I wanted to breathe in his fresh newborn scent, to count his toes and let his fingers curl around mine. I wanted to nurse him, to allow my body to nourish his.

I wanted to enjoy him. But he was four stories down surrounded by nurses and doctors in a plastic protective warmer covered with wires and tubes.

Where were the debut Facebook pictures of us holding him? Where were the balloons? Where was the celebration? Just hearing someone say "congratulations" would have added a different perspective. Everyone around us either walked on eggshells or gave us condolences, which compounded our grief.

We waited for answers, but the doctors couldn't give us any. They simply didn't know. Christian's cleft palate case was one of the worst they'd ever seen; there was no way to prepare us for the diagnosis.

In the midst of despair we had to make a choice. Does God determine the course of our spiritual walk or do our circumstances? For a while circumstances defined mine.

When I was finally allowed to hold Christian, I marveled at the scene in the NICU. The air smelled sterile. Clean. Windows lined each of the tiny private rooms, complete with two chairs, an incubator, and various other machines. Most of the babies, many of them preemies, were so small they could fit in the palm of your hand. Wires crisscrossed the incubators like mesh netting, and machines hummed and beeped.

Does God determine the course of our spiritual walk or do our circumstances?

Christian looked so tiny and helpless, yet compared to his other NICU-cellmates, he was a normal, healthy size.

Normal.

Loathed word; desired situation.

If our life was normal, I'd be rocking him in his nursery at home. If our life was normal, we'd be snuggled on the couch, watching TV as Christian nestled on my chest. If our life was normal, we'd have a sink full of dirty bottles and a diaper pail ready for a trip to the curb.

I would have traded *anything* to have that kind of normal.

For the first time I clearly understood the degree of difference between how God sees us and how we judge others. Man looks at the outward appearance, but God looks at the heart. (See 1 Samuel 16:7.) I realized everyone would see Christian's disfigurement as the sum of who he was, but not me. I *knew* this baby. He was somebody to me, with a temperament and personality still to be discovered.

It wasn't until I became a parent that I understood what it means when God says that we are His children and He loves us like a father. My heart was so full of passion and protectiveness for my baby, an overwhelming combination of emotions I'd never experienced until that moment. As I gazed at my child's broken face, anger crept to the surface. His outward appearance didn't accurately reflect the pureness and perfection of his soul.

DARK DIAGNOSIS

For the next few days we navigated a fog of doctors, assessments, questions, forms, tests. The helplessness I felt on the C-section table was nothing compared to the desperation that crept in as specialist after specialist walked away with no answers.

On the fourth day Christian had his first surgery to insert a feeding tube. We'd been at the hospital all day, sick with worry while our newborn was given anesthesia. During the wait Chris and I alternated holding each other's hands and having quiet moments to ourselves. The seconds crawled by.

I struggled with my emotions toward God. I hated the hardships Christian endured those first few days of life and dreaded the extensive obstacles ahead. Didn't God care about him?

The evening of Christian's first surgery we were hit with the first round of answers. However, it couldn't have happened at a worse time for us. Emotionally we were completely drained from the day. Raw.

I had gone to a private room to pump milk for Christian's nightly feedings. When I returned to Christian's room, Chris was sobbing. I rushed over and laid my hand on his shoulder while peering into Christian's bassinet and checking his monitors.

"What's wrong?" I said.

"A doctor came in and basically said, 'Your son is blind. Sorry,' and walked out."

Your son is blind. Sorry. Drop the mic.

While Christian reacted to a light, he couldn't see. Christian's eyes had never formed.

Because the side of his face had been connected to the placenta, he literally couldn't turn his head in utero. The ultrasounds hadn't revealed this because Jennifer was never able to get clear views of the placental edge and Christian's face.

Yet no one had *said* anything.

To hear it out loud from Chris's lips was terrible. That he'd heard it from a doctor while he was alone was heartbreaking. He stared at his hands, allowing the tears to fall without shame.

Together we mourned while the world bustled and beeped around us.

Where was God in this?

On the way home that night the weight of the news combined with the exhaustion, grief, and stress proved too much for Chris. He hallucinated on the drive home, which frightened me. He swerved a few times to avoid obstacles in the road, yet the streets were clear. It's crazy how when one person falls, the other person musters strength from some deep recess.

"What you're seeing isn't there," I assured him before we switched places, but I was one piece of bad news away from a breakdown myself.

Questions, Answers, and More Questions

After almost two months of waiting for a complete diagnosis, answers came from our plastic surgeon. There are so many incredible people in Christian's life, but his plastic surgeon is an extra special hero. He is compassionate and tactful, unlike the doctor who dropped the "your baby is blind" bomb then ran to escape any emotional shrapnel.

While we sat in the NICU with Christian, his plastic surgeon uploaded a diagram on his computer and patiently explained our son's condition. He had been born with parts of his face missing, even the right side of his skull next to his eye. The diagnosis: an extremely rare case of Tessier cleft palate, classifications 3, 4, and 5, which refer to the extent of the cleft and where it is located on the face. Less than sixty documented cases of Christian's condition have ever been reported.[1]

The relief of *finally* having an answer, a specific diagnosis, both overwhelmed and freed us. At last we could create a plan to get Christian the proper care. His plastic surgeon explained that it would take dozens of surgeries to fully close the roof of his mouth and replace the bone.

Yet in the midst of those emotions of relief, the anger hit full force. When I was pregnant, I'd been happy simply that Christian was alive. Each ultrasound and healthy heartbeat proved my baby was a fighter and was going to make it. I had trusted God, and He gave us the *worst* possible outcome.

All I could think was, "God, *what* are You doing?" This wasn't the way it was supposed to happen.

I felt powerless. And angry. Hadn't I been good? Hadn't I done what I was supposed to do? I went to church, led praise and worship, taught Sunday school, and now I was in a situation where people were giving me charity and pity. As I watched Christian struggle to survive, I wrestled with God.

You promise, God. You say that nothing can separate us from the love of Christ Jesus our Lord.[2] *Then how come my child was born like this and no one knows why?*

If You love me so much, why are You allowing me to go through this?

You say that we are fearfully and wonderfully made.[3] *Then why do we get bombarded with negative comments? Why do people think Christian's life is not worth living?*

Why, God? Why do You let bad things happen to good people?

You say You work all things together for the good of those who love You,[4] *but this is a nightmare. My life does not look like You are working things out for our good.*

This is where my heart took its darkest turn in my entire life: *If this is Your goodness, God, I don't want any part of it.*

TROUBLE AT HOME

Chris and I were not getting along during this time. He worked as many hours as he could to bring in extra money and possibly to avoid arguments with me. We hardly saw each other those days. I raced to the hospital every morning and studied every spare minute I could find. When I left the hospital, I drove to law school and the next few evening hours were spent in tort law and contracts.

Not only were we apart all the time, we each handled Christian's diagnosis in completely different ways. I was the fighter, and Chris became hands-off. I felt his portion of the weight was added to my shoulders. It crushed me emotionally, and I felt buried by the pressure. We weren't partners. We were barely friends.

Our days melded into one giant ball of exhaustion. The hospital discharged me after a few days of recovery, but Christian stayed. Walking into our house without my baby wasn't the plan, and it took every bit of strength to step through the front door.

As I passed Christian's nursery, I placed a hand on the doorframe. For a moment I imagined him in his crib, gurgling and cooing. A lump formed in my throat, and I barely made it to my bed before bursting into tears.

Even though I was on maternity leave, I was still in the middle of law school. I studied whenever I could, but the majority of my time was spent in the NICU with Christian. I needed my baby and he needed me. How could it be any other way?

When things go wrong, we need to trust God to carry us through. I was angry with God, so I blindly put my trust in the doctors.

This turned out to be a mistake.

If I could go back in time, I would have shaken my shoulders, slapped my cheek, and splashed water on my face. *Wake up, Lacey! You don't have time for pity. You don't have time for grief. You have to learn everything you can so you can make informed decisions.*

I was weak because I wasn't allowing God to get near my heart.

Knowing the next step for Christian's care would have helped me feel more in control of these scary circumstances. Instead I remained in a daze, ignoring the wealth of knowledge at my fingertips. My advice to everyone dealing with a devastating or tragic situation: educate yourself and pray that God will lead you to make the right choices.

It's my biggest regret that I didn't.

Christian's medical decisions were made by the doctors and specialists with no input from me or Chris. When I finally found my voice, I'd already put Christian through procedures that could have waited and allowed him to suffer after a surgery when the staff wouldn't give him the proper pain relief. While I'm grateful that Christian has no memory of this early part of his life, it's scarred forever in my heart.

Life became a tailspin, and our marriage buckled under the pressure. Work. Christian. School. Christian. Study. Christian. Sleep. Christian. My plate overflowed, and I wondered where God was in the midst of my nightmare.

LISTENING FOR GOD

Sometimes spiritual change happens gradually, but God's voice struck me hard during a quiet moment on my lunch break. The smell of lunch lingered through the day care center, mixing with the oddly comforting smell of freshly wiped tables and bleached toys.

Music played in the other room while the little ones took their nap. The soft darkness hugged me. Peaceful and quiet. Fresh. Calm.

Alone for the first time that day, and in between bites, I had a one-sided talk with God: "I demand an answer, God. You need to tell me right now why this is happening. You can't just do this to me. If You're *so good*, then explain Yourself."

My childish ultimatum was really my soul begging Him for an answer.

The music flowed from the other side of the center. Laura Story's "Blessings" came on, the song she wrote when her husband was diagnosed with cancer. The song she wrote out of her grief. The song that squeezed my soul.

I heard God distinctly:

> I don't have to explain *why* right now, and you need to be
> OK even if you *never* know why. I am God. You. Are. Not.
> You prayed for this child. You asked Me to let him live.
> And.
> I.
> Did.
> I gave you a gift, yet you act like he is a *burden*.

Suddenly I was in the eye of the storm, a small respite, like God pushed the pause button on my life. Christian was *not* my burden; he was my *blessing*. It was as if God said to me, "Christian is My love for you on display."

I'll never forget those words He pressed into my heart. The anger evaporated.

I had no idea what we were in store for, how many surgeries, doctor's visits, and therapies we would undergo. I definitely didn't know how I was going to survive the extreme hatred that bubbled forth from strangers when they saw my son. And yet, from that day on, and still to this day, that anger never returned.

I prayed for God to spare my child's life while I was pregnant. He did. Christian was a living, breathing answer to prayer. His life was infinitely precious, and through this one-sided battle with God I glimpsed how much God loved me as His child. He was willing to let me throw an internal temper tantrum to release the ugliness stored in my heart. My brokenness was acceptable. My misguided anger was not.

SEEING POSITIVES

God shows us His graciousness through Christian every day. He's an active, healthy little boy who has his own set of superpowers. For example, when you're blind, your other senses are heightened. When Christian enters a room, he automatically takes a little sniff. Even at a very young age he quickly identified when he was at a doctor's office and promptly burst into tears when we'd walk in the door.

He's also incredibly gifted musically. We were blessed to have a piano teacher work with him, and at the age of two Christian could pound out the opening of "Für Elise." He loves to listen to his headphones, and I'm so grateful that we don't use VCRs anymore. We replay Elmo on YouTube constantly. He has an unusual capacity to sit quietly for a lengthy period of time while he listens to stories or feel the textures of special books.

We were fully prepared for him to be born with mental deficiencies, so another blessing is that speech and taste are our main focuses. Though we are slowly working through developmental milestones, Christian is extremely intelligent. Our therapists and doctors are always surprised at how quickly he learns, and after he recovered from his palate surgery, he began saying all the words he knew but couldn't form.

I'm always surprised when people ask me how I can be happy all the time. They just don't know. I didn't used to be this way. I learned to see God through the tragedies. He is *always* working things out for us. Faith means that while we won't always understand why things happen, we can trust that God is *always* good.

Chapter Three

FOR BETTER OR
FOR WORSE

A wedding is an event, but marriage is a life.
—Myles Munroe, *Waiting and Dating*

I MET CHRIS AND Jesus on the same day. While I believed in God and the Bible, my parents didn't really go to church, so I hadn't spent much time in one. I'd felt the calling to give my life to Jesus since I was nine years old, but my family thought I was too young. So when my friend Jeanette asked me to come with her to church on April 4, 2002, I said yes.

Chris sat on one side of the small building, staring intently at the preacher. My friend and I sat on the other side, staring intently at him. We were convinced he was at least twenty-two years old, which to our fifteen-year-old selves was a huge deal. We joked about how old he was, and I wondered how old I'd have to be before he'd date me.

Thankfully I'm a good multitasker because while my heart beat wildly over Chris's gorgeous blue eyes, my soul responded to the good news of Jesus. I gave my life to Christ that day and was never the same.

Two weeks later the members of our tiny congregation drove to the creek for a baptism celebration. Pastor Higgins baptized several members of the congregation that sunny day, and as I stood dripping wet on the bank, I watched Chris emerge from the water as a new man.

I started attending youth group because, well, that's where I'd find Jesus and boys. My older brother, Dustin, started coming and became friends with Chris, who *thank goodness* was only seventeen. When we'd go on youth trips, I made sure I was available to sit next to him—or basically be in the vicinity of wherever he and my brother were.

One June afternoon Dustin and I were hanging out at Chris's house when my brother started acting super funny.

"Go ahead, Chris," he said.

"What? What!" Chris responded.

"Do it," said Dustin. And back and forth, back and forth. I pretended to ignore them, until my brother went out onto the front porch. "Hey guys, come out here," he called.

Chris and I scampered out. Dustin retreated in.

And locked us out.

He peered through the curtains like a weirdo and yelled, "You can't come back in until you ask her, Chris."

So. Incredibly. Awkward.

Chris is a talker once you get to know him, but he suddenly became super shy. I didn't care. I liked him a lot, and obviously my brother knew something I had only dreamed about. So I waited.

Chris kicked at the porch beams as he shifted his weight from one foot to the other, scuffing the bottom of his shoe against the rough wood.

"I wanted to ask you out, but I was nervous." He looked up at me. "You're so pretty, Lacey."

I melted.

And that was it. My brother takes credit for getting us together, but I attribute the Chris and Lacey story to Jeanette because she had the courage to invite me to church. Not only did God save my soul, but He also gave me my soul mate.

Dating Chris was exciting. We were complete opposites in a lot of ways, which added intrigue and excitement. I'm the romantic, gushy type, and Chris is a "man's man," a macho guy. He's never been all foo-foo, tossing rose petals on the bed. I'd tease, "You need to serenade me!" and he'd just say, *"Mm hmm,"* and wink at me.

He is also a realist. Once we were in the car, and I said, "You'd argue with me just to argue. You'd say the sky wasn't blue." Bad timing on my part. He looked out at the rain-heavy clouds. "Well," he said, "it's actually more gray."

Yet we had a great time together. He makes me feel comfortable, he's stable, and despite his serious demeanor, he has an amazing sense of humor. Chris understands the concept of family and sacrifice because he knows what it's like to be neglected. He carries strength on his shoulders and experience in his eyes. He is a survivor. A fighter.

I knew he'd be an amazing father to our children, and I was right. When it comes to his sons, there's nothing that man won't do.

SMALL-TOWN FUN

When you grow up in a place like Woodbury, Tennessee (population 2,500, three gas stations, and a McDonald's), you find all kinds of creative ways to have fun. Youth group activities were always a blast, our friends hosted parties, and we'd go to the movies or hang out in the Walmart parking lot.

Don't judge. #SmallTowns

Chris worked various jobs after high school, and I went down the college track—*Go Middle Tennessee State Blue Raiders*. I played intramural volleyball in college, so after the games we'd head over to Applebee's to nosh on half-priced appetizers. There was always something to do, and we had a great time together, even though people often thought he was my dad. He looked five years older than he was, and it didn't help that I looked like I was twelve.

Lacey Buchanan
December 11, 2009

So close to graduation that I can smell it! And it smells like "wonderful"!

One day during my senior year of high school Chris and I were at the creek on a church swim outing. The church's strict rules on modesty prevented me from wearing my swimsuit. This was a major disappointment since I looked super cute in it, so I chose a dark T-shirt and shorts. We waded in the creek and I splashed Chris a few times, then fought back when he tried to throw me in. I braved the deeper area when I felt a sharp pinch and a slimy object brush my leg.

And. I. Screamed.

I rushed to the bank, blood pouring from four pinhole marks. Chris rushed me to the ER, and surprisingly the staff let him come into the exam room. A nurse walked into the room with my chart, said hello to me, and then turned to Chris, "Are you the dad?"

Ummm…that's my boyfriend, and he's only seventeen!

We thought it was hilarious, and thankfully I had no reaction to the snake bite. We would have tried to see if Chris could get alcohol without an ID, but neither one of us tapped into our rebellious streaks. Our days passed happily and the future was clear.

DREAMS FOR THE FUTURE

Instead of buying me an engagement ring, Chris bought me a house. We didn't really have a formal engagement moment. It was obvious to both of us that we'd found our life partner. Our conversations easily turned to the future, and we dreamed of owning a home and having a house full of babies.

Chris and I had been casually looking for a place, and as things go, a friend of ours knew a lady who lived a few houses down from my parents who was thinking of selling. The house wasn't on the market yet, but once she was ready, we met her at the lawyer's office, signed some papers, and Chris moved in.

The hunt for my wedding dress began a week later. I found a fabulous gown in the four-figure price range, but the thought of spending that much money hit my frugal self pretty hard. It was a beautiful drop-waist number, with a lace halter V-neck top, a ribbon encircling my hips, and an ivory skirt with a flowing train. We went to David's Bridal to see if we could find the same style for a better price. The saleswoman took note of what I was looking for, and before I knew it, I was slipping in and out of crinoline and lace.

When I put on the strapless A-line with champagne trim across the top and a diamond-shaped ruffle pattern on the skirt, I knew it was the one. It fit me beautifully, caressing my curves in a modest yet feminine manner. Best part—it was on sale.

My bridesmaids tried on a few different dresses, and after we giggled that the banana dress would be the perfect accent color, we settled on strapless A-line dresses that mimicked mine in the same champagne color as my trim.

With the dresses ordered, we filled our days with decorations, flower arrangements, and cake-tasting heaven. My best friends threw me a bachelorette party complete with limo service to downtown Nashville.

 Lacey Buchanan
June 30, 2008

Enjoying the married life!

THE BIG DAY

Even though Chris and I had been together for six years, my stomach was all in butterflies. I couldn't wait to see his face when I appeared at the end of the aisle.

For our late-afternoon wedding I chose my accessories carefully, settling on teardrop pearl earrings and a coordinating pearl necklace and bracelet. A friend applied my makeup, creating a soft smoky eye, and pinned the veil just below the crown of my silky golden hair.

Chris looked incredible in a white tuxedo with champagne and ivory tie.

My oversized bouquet was a mix of lilies, roses, and small white buds, contrasting beautifully with the dark green leaves and stems. My bridesmaids carried nosegays in the same flower combination.

David Higgins, the same pastor who preached that Sunday six years before when I gave my life to Jesus, performed the ceremony under a flower-laden gazebo. Chris and I pledged our love and commitment before our friends and family, and when he kissed the bride, our guests erupted into cheers.

Our reception was held in The Corner, a wood-paneled hall we'd decorated with crisp white tablecloths, draped tulle across the ceiling, flower centerpieces, and wooden Bs placed in the round windows. The cake drew *oohs* and *aahs*, stacked four layers high with sugared calla lilies and roses climbing up each layer.

We danced the night away then drove to Chattanooga for our first night as husband and wife. The next day we flew to Saint Petersburg, Florida, where we basked in the sun's glow on the gorgeous white sand beaches and celebrated our new life together.

We returned home tanned and relaxed, eager to begin the daily life of a married couple. I was excited to move into our house. Our home.

The days flowed in easy companionship. I enjoyed my job at the day care center where I played with the little ones and came home without any stress or busywork. Conversely Chris worked a lot of hours, often coming home after dark, but the overtime gave us a great start. I loved making him dinner, and even daily chores like laundry and washing dishes made me feel domestic and wifey.

We were carefree and fun-loving during these "for better" times. The first two years of marriage passed quickly.

We found out I was pregnant shortly after I got accepted into law school. Both these paths were amazing wins for our family. Our pregnancy story isn't typical, and thankfully those hard times brought us closer together as we clung to each other for support. Unfortunately those hard times after Christian was born pushed us apart.

A ROCKY ROAD

Things got a bit rocky for us after we had Christian. Personally I became obsessed with Christian's care, and my world was flooded with demands, decisions, and appointments. I merely survived that first month, a shell of the woman Chris knew and loved.

Date nights were nonexistent while Christian was in the NICU. I got home late every night and left first thing in the morning. Once our baby was home with us, Chris and I expected to have more time together, that we'd rekindle the flame. But romance became an illusion.

Time after time we were unable to find someone to watch Christian, so date nights became a thing of the past. It's completely understandable that Christian's condition left people a little wary. I was the only person who had been trained with his machines. Even my sweet parents were terrified they'd do something wrong if I wasn't there to be able to quickly fix a mistake. We were both so exhausted that even a fast-food dinner eaten in the parking lot would have been a treat.

What we do for each other before marriage is no indication of what we will do after marriage.[1]

Because of our differing schedules Chris and I were two ships passing in the night. I juggled Christian's schedule (a full-time job in and of itself) and tried to balance law school and my job on top of everything else. I needed my husband's help, but Christian's condition frightened him.

Our responsibilities were no longer split, but I didn't know how to tell Chris what I needed him to do, and he didn't know how to help. In his defense, he literally wasn't available to take

Christian to appointments, so he always got news secondhand when I'd come home and share what new insights I'd been told.

We were opposites in how we handled our new reality: I was a fighter; he was a flight-er. I became consumed and obsessed: filled out the paperwork, made the phone calls, stayed on hold, scheduled appointments, drove to therapies, listened to diagnoses, researched procedures, ordered supplies, studied for law school, attended classes, and went to work. For whatever reason I tried to protect Chris from things that he didn't need protection from. It was polarizing for both of us, so he backed off.

Even when Christian was first born, Chris hesitated to hold him. He was nervous around babies anyway, and the crisscrossed tubes and wires made Christian appear more fragile than he was. Chris would lean over the incubator, hold his hand, and tell him how much he loved him and that everything was going to be OK, but it wasn't until Christian was almost two weeks old that Chris wrapped his arms around him.

Chris's reaction to our child having a serious disability was to not deal with it. Head in the sand. *If I can't see it, it's not there.* To cope, he emotionally retreated, which left me front and center carrying the job of both parents. He was happy to let me handle everything, including the media frenzy, preferring not to be involved or participate in family events. Stepping away made it hurt less, so he provided for our family the only way he knew how—by engrossing himself in his job.

In his defense, this avoidance is how he had always handled pain or ugly situations. He'd seen people close to him do the same, pretending problems didn't exist. And he was criticized if he tried to do things any other way. Avoidance was what he'd always known. He'd never learned how to deal with negative circumstances in a healthy way.

While I tried to give him the benefit of the doubt, I still felt rejected. And angry. I needed him more than ever, and he pulled away. My heart shattered, and I needed God to salvage the wreckage.

On top of the other struggles Chris and I faced, we were in survival mode financially. If babies come with expensive price tags, the cost for babies with disabilities is astronomical. It was important to us that I stay home with Christian, but we couldn't survive on Chris's income alone. We crunched the numbers time and time again, but we were a two-income family that needed the financial resources of a five- or ten-income family.

For the first eighteen months of Christian's life I juggled the heavy workload of his care, school, and my job at the day care center, and prayed for a respite. We crunched the numbers over and over again. Chris felt an enormous amount of pressure to provide for his family. He left for work early, stayed late, and accepted every extra shift he could. I was desperate for a break, eager to quit working and be Christian's full-time caregiver, but Chris refused to budge. We couldn't make ends meet if I quit, so tension grew.

Something had to give, and it wouldn't be Christian or anything to do with his care. I resented Chris for not providing me with an escape or taking some of the workload off my shoulders. Regardless of Chris's objections, I faced the reality of quitting my job or quitting law school. My cheery home full of promises and light became dark and dreary.

Instead of enjoying life, I zombied my way through. Exhausted. Emotional. Every night I closed my eyes and reviewed the next day's agenda. And every night I doubted that I'd have the strength to make it through.

LOVING MORE

Christian was born in February, and my first year of law school ended in May. I was eager to begin my second year and get to the halfway point. I left work and drove an hour out to the school to register. About thirty minutes down the highway, I spotted a commotion in the middle of the road. Before I knew what happened, the driver of the car in front of me slammed on the brakes.

Vehicles aren't designed to go from sixty to zero in a split second. I gripped the steering wheel and punched the brake and skidded into the car in front of me. The impact knocked me back and pulled me forward; my seatbelt felt hot against my neck from the friction.

Stunned, I tried to focus on the scene in front of me. Men were in the middle of the road, grabbing sheet rock that had fallen from their truck. The car I'd hit was not the only car that had suddenly braked trying to avoid hitting the men, and several cars were stopped on the side as they waited until it was safe to get back on the road.

If you rear-end someone in Tennessee, it's your fault no matter what. By the time the cops arrived, the people who'd indirectly caused the accident by not properly fastening their sheet rock had fled the scene.

Thank God Christian wasn't in the car.

My car was destroyed, so I called the tow company and Chris, who left work early to get me to the school. When he arrived, he threw his arms around me and squeezed me tightly, despite how sweaty I was from being in the sun for almost an hour. He drove me to the school, and I found his presence calming and reassuring. We didn't feel like partners, but our feelings aren't always an accurate pulse of the relationship.

We arrived at the law school, and I was eager to pay for my

classes and get home. It had been a long day, and I was ready to hug Christian and get started on my nightly chores so I could crash into bed.

"I'm afraid we have a problem," the registrar said.

Oh no.

Turns out that while I'd done great in my classes, I'd failed the third section of one class. Coincidentally this portion was during Christian's month-long stay in the hospital and two surgeries. I had to retake my entire first year.

Oh no... no... no.

Couldn't I just repeat the class I failed? Isn't it ridiculous to pay for classes I'd passed? I should receive credit for those.

The registrar, however, refused to budge. I should have known by her hair—the severer the bun, the stricter the woman.

My nerves were already on high alert from the embarrassment and frustration of the accident. Hot tears welled in my eyes, but I refused to let them fall. I hadn't fought so hard and spent so many nights studying to have to redo everything.

Didn't they realize I was hanging on by a thread here? Passing any class during this time was a miracle, and I'd passed several. Shouldn't I be rewarded for that?

It wasn't worth it.

I couldn't do this again.

I definitely wasn't paying to retake classes I'd already passed.

"Fine," I told her. "Give me back my tuition check."

She looked down her glasses at me. "Why don't you take some time to think about it?"

I almost leaped over the counter.

Chris grabbed my shoulders and steered me away from the window. He settled me into a scratchy gray chair in the lobby, then sat across from me and put a hand on my knee.

"Lacey, I know how hard this is, and I totally understand that you want to quit. But you're going to make an amazing lawyer. We can get through this." He gave my leg a squeeze and waited.

Fairy tales get some things wrong, and one of those lessons is this: it isn't the flowers or diamonds that make you fall in love; it's these simple gifts of encouragement. I knew Chris was right. This stupid system wasn't going to stop me.

I retook my course and passed. Then despite the registrar's edict, I dropped the other first-year classes I had registered for and started law school year number two.

Just as He made a way for me to continue law school without retaking the entire first year, God showed Chris and me a way forward in our marriage. No marriage is perfect, but we were struggling. There were times when we both thought it would be easier if we said, "Let's be done with this." But we both wanted to make sure that if our marriage ended, it wasn't because we hadn't done everything we could to save it.

Counseling provided a way for us to share our feelings without pointing fingers. It gave us quality time to listen, understand, and be heard. We showered each other with grace and forgiveness. Once we acknowledged our shortcomings, we recommitted to purposefully work on our relationship daily.

Dealing with a disabled child adds a new dimension to the marriage, and we believe that marriages can be restored regardless of the obstacles. It's silly to pretend our marriage is perfect—it helps no one to fake it. I feel totally inadequate to give marriage advice, but I've learned that marriage is a whole lot of dying to yourself. If you can't do that, you probably shouldn't get married.

Following God doesn't guarantee a life without trouble, and it doesn't guarantee a stress-free marriage. In fact, Jesus warns us that there will be trouble in this world. Chris and I have decided to trust that since He overcame the world, He can help us build a strong foundation together. For better or for worse.

Chapter Four

TESTS, TRIALS, AND TEARS

*Outward pressure is always an opportunity to be
inwardly transformed.*
—LISA BEVERE, *GIRLS WITH SWORDS*

THERE'S A NATURAL order to birth: Push. Breathe. Push.
Breathe. Push. Here's your baby.

In theory it's not difficult, but as many mothers can
attest, that beautiful little birth plan gets thrown out the window
the moment something happens in the delivery room. And something almost always happens.

Because of his disabilities Christian spent the first twenty-eight
days of his life in the neonatal intensive care unit at our hospital.
Instead of resting in his cozy bassinette next to my bed, he slept
in an incubator warmed by lights. Instead of his room being seconds away from mine, it was over an hour's drive one-way.

Despite how much I wanted him home, the NICU allowed

doctors and specialists to access Christian at all hours. So we swallowed our disappointment, endured the long drives, and prayed for answers.

LOSS OF CONTROL

When our baby was taken to the NICU immediately after he was born, I experienced a feeling of loss of control. My arms ached for my child, the soul that my body nurtured, protected, and loved for nine months. I felt incomplete, certain that danger flirted with my baby. The hollowness that followed was almost unbearable.

My brain was on high alert. All I could think about was getting to Christian.

My C-section recovery left me at the mercy of the hospital staff. A few moments after he was born, Christian was shown to me above the drapery for a few precious seconds. I wanted to know what was happening, but I was strapped to the operating table while doctors stitched me up and pushed pain medication through my veins.

I was jealous that I didn't get to hold him. I longed for him.

For the first eight hours I had no idea what was going on and literally no way to get help. Standing, or even sitting for that matter, after a C-section is ridiculous. I'd call the NICU nurses' station for updates—"How is he? Is he being fed? What's going on? Do they know what's wrong?"

Almost every time I heard a simple, "He's fine."

He's fine?

I knew from Chris's description that my sweet baby was not *fine*, but what could I do? Short of Chris carrying me downstairs, gown flapping in the wind as the IV pump rolled behind us, I had to wait.

As soon as I was able to get on my feet for the few precious seconds it takes to get into a wheelchair, Chris wheeled me to the NICU to see Christian for the first time. The monitor's steady beeps indicated he was medically stable as he lay in the warming unit.

At first all I could see were the tubes that ran all over his body. He looked fragile to me, even though he was a healthy size compared to many of the other sweet preemies bundled in their own incubators.

I became the mom of the child no one knew how to deal with. Christian didn't fit the typical NICU baby needs. While the doctors and nurses assessed and tested, my instincts screamed, "He needs *me*."

My baby shouldn't be lying in the incubator; he should be in my arms. I begged to hold him. He was medically stable with no signs of distress or need for medical intervention. However, I wasn't *allowed* to hold him or feed him until the next day.

After I insisted, the staff permitted me to hold my baby for the first time—for fifteen minutes *max*. A nurse carefully rescued Christian from beneath the web of wires. She carefully maneuvered and wrapped the IV and other tubes attached to him so they wouldn't snag on anything. She adjusted the cords and tubes to ensure they remained connected to the machines. I sat patiently as she placed him in my arms.

For a few precious moments I memorized every inch of my baby boy's face.

He turned his head when I murmured in his ear. I whispered how much I loved him as I stroked his cheek, his head, his fingers. Two long strips of gauze were taped over his eyes, yet crimson tissue peeked out of both ends. The right side of his skull disconnected from the middle of his face, creating an island with his nose. The severity of the cleft palate turned his lips into a permanent grin.

He was the most beautiful baby in the world.

The nurse returned, but I held on to Christian until the last possible second. Obligingly I allowed her to slip him out of my arms after the quickest fifteen minutes of my life.

Christian's condition baffled the doctors and stumped the specialists, and I was merely the life-giving vessel who couldn't help fix him. It often felt like I was an unnecessary fixture in the NICU, in the way unless a consent form needed my signature. I pumped breast milk, although they would have substituted formula just as easily. I was a signature-generating machine, as simple as that.

This became our pattern: See. Pray. Leave. We caught only glimpses of Christian between the bustle of patterned scrubs and white lab coats.

Because Christian's case was so rare, no one, including the medical staff, really knew how to handle our situation or how to talk to us. I yearned for the mother-child bonding experience, so Chris and I visited Christian together multiple times a day. Recovering from a C-section by itself is exhausting, so we'd make our way up and down, up and down, from the NICU to my hospital room, as many times as I could handle.

We'd pass other rooms on the maternity floor, and I envied each mom whose baby was allowed to be in her room. It should have been our story. I complained to God in my heart each time we punched the elevator buttons to go see our son.

THE GENEROSITY OF FRIENDS

The NICU has strict policies regarding visitors. Two people were allowed in at a time, and one of them had to be either Chris or myself. We'd check in, scrub up to our elbows at the washing station, and if the nurse on duty smelled cigarette smoke or too much perfume, a gown was required over the clothing.

If it was Chris's turn to bring a visitor to see Christian, I stayed in the waiting area with the rest of the group, and vice versa.

Our friends and family provided a lot of comfort in those early days. They wished us well, held our hands, and prayed for us. Our church members called and checked in on us, especially on the weekends. When people rearrange their hectic schedules to come to the hospital, it is such an act of love. It may have been only an hour out of their day, but it meant the world to us.

The generosity of our friends and family was a double-edged sword. As difficult as it is to say, we were mourning not the loss of a child but the loss of a *typical* child. It's hard to know what to do in these situations. How do you show how much your heart is breaking?

... for some of us, one mile can be more to walk than thirty.[1]

One friend brought balloons and whispered, "Congrats," in my ear as she hugged me. I wanted more of that, for our friends and family to be excited that we'd brought a precious life into the world. I know they were, and I know saying congratulations may have felt patronizing, like they would be cheering for the disability, the numerous surgeries, and the astronomical medical expenses. Hooray.

The experience gave me tremendous insight into how people feel when they're directly dealing with a struggle. I realized that I'd often not done enough for others, and I vowed to change that. I want to pay forward the kindness we received from loved ones and strangers alike.

Sometimes God's gifts aren't tangible. They come in the form of compassion and friendship when you're in a dark place emotionally. The outpouring of love from friends and family wasn't how I expected God to heal part of my heart, but it was exactly what I needed, and it was more valuable than any present.

After spending a short amount of time with Christian, our friends would come out of the NICU, their eyes filled with tenderness and tears. There's no handbook for this, so we expressed ourselves honestly. The truth is that this situation wasn't anything close to ideal.

I understood exactly what their tears meant. I was sorry too.

Desperately I wished I could have said, "At least he's healthy," but I couldn't because we didn't know exactly what was wrong. Thus I draped my soul in black, became strong for our visitors, and masked my grief through the early days that felt more like a funeral than a birth.

Lacey Buchanan
May 29, 2011

I think that through my trials I have complained a little too much, and I have decided that I am going to find things to be thankful for, even when I feel like complaining.

Feeling Helpless

Eventually it was time for me to go home. The hospital needed my bed for the next expectant mother, and I had healed enough to leave. I packed slowly. Toothbrush. Extra clothes. Hair brush. Christian's coming home outfit was still neatly folded in my travel bag.

As I stood up out of the wheelchair to get into the car, I glanced at Christian's empty car seat and the diaper bag sitting next to it. It felt wrong to leave Christian there, but I felt completely helpless; I couldn't even stand up on my own without help. I'd complained about a ten-minute walk to the NICU, but the distance between my baby and me was now growing to over an hour's drive time. I wished more than anything to be traveling down only a few flight of stairs to get to him.

Chris and I cried the entire way home. With each one of the sixty-plus miles, the pain of being away from Christian built up in my heart and knotted my stomach. I'd grown to love and hate this drive—every morning I couldn't wait to get to my son, but each evening the road beckoned to me and I hated that I had to answer its call.

Chris was off that week, and after I was discharged, we drove together every day to the hospital. When he went back to work, I began my lonely hour-and-a-half commute to see my baby. I'd grab some coffee and breakfast, stay in Christian's room all day, then head home after dark with just enough energy to give Chris a tired kiss good night and fall into bed.

Every three hours I woke up to pump breast milk and call the hospital to check on Christian. I'd barely fall asleep after the last pumping session before the alarm went off and the process started all over again.

While we had several issues while in the NICU, the hospital did offer to let me stay in one of the rooms specifically for families who lived far away. It was a sweet gesture. Our finances were getting a little tight, and there were times I wondered if I'd be able to afford driving a total of three hours each day. However, I'd become acquainted with a couple of other families who lived four and five hours away. Daily visits with their sick babies wasn't an option, so while I longed to be with Christian every hour of the day, I declined.

God blessed that decision. Friends would drop by and bring restaurant and gas gift cards. That was such a help to us. There were times I'd be studying so intently in Christian's room that I'd forget to eat lunch, and cafeteria food can be tolerated for only so long. Being blessed with a McDonald's or Wendy's gift card was a small treat for which I was extremely grateful.

OUR LITTLE SUPERMAN

Having a baby forced me to grow up. I only wish I'd matured a little faster than I did.

The absolute hardest part of having a child in the NICU, besides watching my baby endure tests and surgery, was not being able to *be* Christian's mom. We were told what needed to happen, and as first-time parents walking blindly through this process with the doctors, we didn't know what to do besides sign the papers and pray for answers.

When Christian was hungry, I couldn't run into the kitchen and make a bottle or even hold him close to me and breast-feed. I wasn't the decision maker. I wasn't in charge.

When I arrived at the NICU in the mornings, the night-shift nurse caught me up on what I missed and how Christian's day was going. She filled me in on the schedule for the day before she went home herself.

A part of me daydreamed about racing into the NICU, unplugging Christian from all the monitors, and rushing him home to cuddle him without the beeps and chirps of the monitors. I wanted his first sounds, smells, and touches to be mine, yet we were separated. My heart broke for my child who was receiving the care he needed but not the mother's love I longed to give him.

The IV went away after the first week, which made holding him a lot easier. As the days went by, I learned about the different machines, what they did, how they worked, and most importantly how to stop the alarms when I accidentally pulled on a cord. My confidence grew, and I picked Christian up without the nurses there to supervise. I felt like I was doing something wrong by holding my baby without permission, and I was ready to be admonished at any time.

And yet I knew that the best thing for Christian was for him to be right where he was. He was warm, monitored, and loved, even if he couldn't feel it from the safety of my arms. Even though I hated every second of him not being home with us, of not putting him to sleep in his decorated nursery, or not holding him in the middle of the night, this is what had to be.

Of all the challenges we faced in those first few days, the biggest one was how to feed Christian. With the severity of the cleft palate, Christian couldn't even come close to latching, so breast-feeding was never an option. Specialists tried a bottle specifically created for children with cleft palates. It didn't work.

Our only other option was to insert a nasogastric tube (NG tube) down his throat to his stomach. However, at three days old Christian pulled the tube out. Repeatedly. And each time the nurses reinserted the tube, they ran the risk of inserting it into his lungs rather than his stomach.

After more deliberation the doctors decided Christian would be better off with a feeding tube in his stomach. The catch? This tube required surgery.

We were still overwhelmed and in a state of exhaustion when the medical team gave us their spiels. "This is what's going to happen. This is what they're going to do. Sign these forms." I felt like we were being pushed and pulled, this way and that way, with no thread of hope to hold on to and no firm ground to stand on.

Was this the right choice? What else could we do? I couldn't let my baby starve.

Our little superman underwent his first surgery at four days old. On February 22, 2011, the medical team carted him from the NICU to the operating room. No procedure is standard when it comes to putting a four-day-old child under anesthesia. I paced the waiting room, unable to focus on anything until a nurse came and told us it was over.

I stayed with Christian the entire day in the NICU after his surgery and slept in a proffered wooden chair that felt like cardboard. He cried constantly, which was understandable after having had surgery, but there was something in his cry that told me more was going on.

It was my first experience with maternal instincts. I knew he was hurting, but my opinions fell on deaf ears. I told every nurse on staff that I thought he needed something, but they assured me he was fine. Babies cry.

But this was different. He was most definitely sore from the abdominal incisions, but I also thought he was hungry. From all the reading I'd done during my pregnancy, I knew that breast-fed babies drank until they were full, often wanting to nurse every two to three hours either due to hunger or for comfort. I'd also read that breast milk is absorbed faster than formula.

Christian's tummy was dependent upon a spreadsheet of data that the nurses followed. Too much food into the feeding tube would cause vomiting, so they trusted the machine to pump the recommended amount of breast milk into his stomach. I understood the logic, but to me the risk of a little spit up was worth it to make sure he felt full and satisfied.

As I listened to his cries, it became clear to me that his hunger was an underlying issue. Yet I wasn't in charge of his feeding, and they wouldn't let me give him any more than the suggested dosages of breast milk.

Two days later my fears were validated. At six days old Christian lost enough weight for them to start him on a calorie fortifier. This wasn't a choice they ran by Chris or me. It was simply done.

It became clear to me that my presence didn't mean a thing. I could have stayed home all day if I'd wanted to. I was angry, exhausted, and tired of being ignored, of following orders but not having a say-so in my child's routine. I needed someone to treat me like his mother and not like an intrusive neighbor.

SOMETHING TO CELEBRATE

We celebrated Christian's one-week birthday with a Happy Birthday balloon and cupcakes. Anyone who entered the NICU was offered a treat. It was our desperate attempt to find a positive after our first week of feeding tubes, surgery, and frustration.

It was also a way to thank the nurses and staff who had been incredible to us. We were at the hospital all the time, so we met almost every nurse who cared for Christian. There were many nurses who were compassionate and caring, but there were some who acted like they were inconvenienced by our presence. When I was around them, I bit my tongue, but I was thinking, "Look, lady. I don't want to be here anymore than you want us here." But it was her *job* to be there.

One night Christian spit up while he was lying on his back. He coughed furiously and I ran to him. The alarms blared and I checked his monitors. Anything below ninety for the oxygen levels was dangerous. When Christian's number hit forty, I felt like I might pass out. I waited for a nurse, but no one came to help us. I was still so new to this motherhood thing that I wasn't sure I was doing everything I needed to do. I mentally pulled myself together, concentrated, and was finally able to clear his airway and calm him down. His levels went back to normal, but mine rose.

As I left for home that night, I stopped the charge nurse. "I have to go home and sleep," I said. "Is this going to happen again? Is my baby safe here?" She assured me Christian would be fine, but I had my doubts as I drove home.

Thankfully some of the nurses were amazing and went above

and beyond to make things easier for us. They took the time to help us understand why certain things were happening, and we remain friends with a few to this day. In fact, one of the social workers helped us file for Social Security insurance, which has time-sensitive submission deadlines, and suggested I start our blog. Her kindness was such a breath of fresh air for us!

One amazing NICU program that the hospital had in place helped our family so much. Each nurse was allowed to become the primary nurse to a child of their choice. It helped form bonds between the staff and the babies, and it did our hearts a world of good.

Christian was blessed with two nurses who chose him as their primary. They not only took a vested interest in Christian, but they were also instrumental in helping me stand up for myself and speak up for my baby. We talked about more than Christian's care. I felt comfortable enough to speak my mind about my fears, anxieties, and what I thought was best for Christian. They respected me as his mom and taught me how to be an advocate for my son.

Their job was to medically take care for Christian, but they emotionally cared for me as well. Nurse Lee taught me that I didn't have to have all the answers; I just had to be willing to look for them. During her shifts she paid extra attention to how I was doing physically and emotionally. She was a mom herself, and she let me share how I was feeling.

When I was overwhelmed with the doctors telling me what we needed to do, she went to the computer and googled. We found the Tennessee School for the Blind that way, along with information about seeing-eye dogs. Those things weren't priorities, but she opened a world of resources to me. I felt more empowered, more sure of myself. Every mom has fears for her kids; Andrea was sweet enough to listen to mine.

The other nurse who played an important role for us was Nurse Michelle. One evening I had packed my bag to head home, but Christian wouldn't stop crying. It was almost nine o'clock, so I rocked him, held his hand, talked to him, sang, soothed, pleaded. No matter what I did, he remained inconsolable. There was no way I could leave with him crying, so I prayed he'd settle down so I could get on the road.

At eleven o'clock he was still upset. I didn't know what to do besides sleep in the rocking chair. At eleven-thirty Michelle came in the room.

"Why don't you go home," she said. "You need rest."

"I can't just leave him."

She looked me square in the eye. "I promise you I'll take care of him. I won't let him lie there and cry."

I weighed my options and knew she was right. I slid my bag onto my shoulder, let my fingers linger on Christian's hand as I said good-bye, then walked out the door. If I didn't go straight to the car, I'd change my mind. Heaven knows I needed to sleep so I could go at full capacity the next day. I got in the car, pulled out of the hospital parking lot, and a sudden peace washed over me.

I got home close to one in the morning and threw myself into bed. Around two o'clock I woke up. There was no noise, nothing to disturb me, but since I was awake, I called Michelle to check in.

"He's been asleep for several hours," she said. "I sat and rocked him until he fell asleep."

For the first time in a long time I had complete and total trust that someone was taking care of my baby the way I would.

PASSING THE TEST

The entire goal of Christian's twenty-eight days in the NICU was to get him home. While it felt like forever to me, there was one sweet baby who had been there for ten months. Heartbreaking.

Christian's first month of life consisted of surgery, blood tests, EKGs, feeding tubes, tests, tests, tests, and tests. The doctors wanted to make sure no other defects had been missed.

They also weren't done with me.

I understood that Christian required special attention and needed constant care. I spent every available second with him, but the hospital added extra requirements that I had to fulfill before they would deign to release him.

It didn't feel like most of the doctors and nurses were trying to partner with us to help us. Instead they handled our situation as if they were granting us some huge favor by doing their jobs, as if they had full parental rights to Christian and we could babysit him if we got a 100 percent on our test.

One of my obligations was to take a baby CPR class, to learn how to use his machines, as well as spend twenty-four hours with Christian under observation to *prove* I could take care of him. I wanted to scream. I cared better for him than some of their staff. Everything I did was for Christian's best interest.

I had no problems taking the class, but I took offense at the control the hospital asserted. I want to be prepared in case of any emergency, but to *prove* my ability to take care of *my* child before I was *allowed* to leave? There are people in this world who are unfit to be parents, but they take their babies home from the hospital every single day, and yet here I was doing a song and dance before the hospital would permit me to have *my baby*.

I felt bitter about our situation, about the extra hassle and obligations we had to perform. But I wanted my baby so desperately I'd have taken fifty classes.

Their attitude galled me, but some of the biggest challenges were headed our way.

I had to be ready.

I *would* be ready.

My baby was coming home.

Chapter Five

STRENGTH IN WEAKNESS

*Faith is not believing in my own unshakable belief. Faith is
believing an unshakable God when everything in me
trembles and quakes.*
—BETH MOORE, *PRAYING GOD'S WORD*

AFTER CHRISTIAN HAD been in the NICU almost a month,
I couldn't wait for him to come home. His nursery was
more than ready, and I looked forward to the midnight
feedings, diaper changes, and the normal mommy-and-baby
daily activities.

God knew what He was doing when He gave us nine months
to prepare for a baby. I'd read all the books, perused online blogs,
and felt certain we were ready for our little man. His nursery was
decked out. Diapers and wipes filled the shelves and the cutest
little outfits were nestled in the drawers.

But no matter how much I thought I knew what life would be

like—*does anyone really sleep when the baby does?*—I definitely wasn't prepared for the total exhaustion that was compounded by mothering a baby with special needs.

HOMECOMING

The day finally arrived! We were going home for good.

My dad used a personal day and came to the hospital to be an extra set of hands. I don't know how I would have managed on my own. The discharge process from the hospital took all day. Sign this. Read that. Initial here.

My dad grabbed a few of my remaining personal items before heading out to bring the car around. I'd stacked a pushcart to the brim with our NICU necessities—no traveling light these days. We didn't make it out to the car until late afternoon, but all I could think was, "Thank God we're getting out of this place."

I held Christian in my arms and an orderly wheeled me to our car. This is not how I'd pictured taking him home. Chris deeply regretted that he couldn't be there, and I wished more than anything that he'd been by my side.

As we left the hospital with Christian securely buckled in his seat for his first car ride, I prayed that the sixty-plus-mile journey would be accident-free. My mom met us at the house, eager to see her grandbaby outside of the tiny NICU room.

Christian was a champion car rider. I was nervous about him getting carsick or being uncomfortable, but he seemed to enjoy it. My dad and I chatted while he drove, but I don't remember the conversation. A surreal feeling blanketed us, like we were leaving one chapter of a fairy tale and headed to the scene where the princess is about to be rescued. Only this time the queen saved her little prince.

We pulled into the driveway, and my mom ran out to meet us. She reached for her grandson and held him while my dad and I unloaded the car. We made several treks to and from the house, but finally all of his equipment was properly organized.

Before I joined my parents in the living room, I carefully removed nine squares of pretty construction paper out of my purse. The nurses had attached die-cut letters spelling out Christian's name across his NICU room window. I arranged them in the proper order and taped them onto his door.

My baby was officially home.

Chris arrived home shortly thereafter. We ordered takeout and spent the evening playing with Christian, marveling at him, thrilled to have him all to ourselves.

I got to be Christian's mom.

I bathed him for the first time outside of a hospital bed and breathed in the sweet scent of newborn shampoo and baby lotion. I dressed him for the first time in one of his many baby shower outfits, tickling his feet before adding socks.

I fed him for the first time on my own with no nurses to back me up if something went wrong. Every mother worries if her baby is getting enough to eat, and I was scared too. My hand trembled as I attached the proper pieces of the feeding tube machine together and measured out the correct dosage. No one else in the family had been trained on how to use the equipment, although *trained* is exaggerating. The nurse gave me a five-minute crash course and that was that. I didn't have a lot of reassurance, but I was counting on a wing and prayer that I got it right.

Seeing God in the Small Things

Four of my six weeks of maternity leave were spent in the NICU, which left me feeling cheated from my bonding time with Christian. We had only two weeks left before I went back to work and someone else would come care for him.

I saw God's love through my boss during this time. She is an amazing woman and offered to let Christian come to the day care with me. It was an incredibly generous offer, but Christian needed constant care, so I wouldn't be able to fulfill my duties if he was there.

The coming home experience was exciting, but reality hit quickly and hard. A positive outcome of Christian being in the NICU was that he was readily available to the doctors. They came to him. Now the situation was reversed, and our long list of appointments and therapies filled the pages of my calendar. Trying to build family time, church, school, study time, chores, work, and relationships around those chunks of time was harder than I'd ever imagined.

None of our friends or family had gone through this before, which made me feel even more alone. I couldn't really vent to anyone. Chris had withdrawn, feeling helpless because he didn't know what to do, so I felt isolated. Honestly I felt like I was drowning in the to-do lists and appointments, so I treaded water, trying to keep my head up. My friendships took a back burner, but the beautiful thing about true friends is that they're always there when you need them, no matter how long you're apart.

I began to look for God in the small things, because that seems to be where He shows up in the biggest ways. A woman from my church brought her daughter over to the house to visit us and hold Christian. They stayed for only a few minutes, but they thoroughly doted on him while they were there.

They sat on the couch, taking turns holding him. Cuddling him. They told me how precious and cute he was, and they truly meant it. This image is permanently etched in my mind because I remember feeling for the first time, "This is how it's supposed to be." Hearing someone *ooh* and *ahh* over my son meant the world because we'd experienced so much of the opposite.

This was definitely a God-moment: the three of us adoring the little baby in the Superman onesie.

SEEDS OF PURPOSE

Organization is one of my superpowers. Our home could easily have become a mini hospital with all of Christian's medical necessities. But the mounds of supplies didn't intimidate me. I thrive on bringing order out of chaos. Give me totes and a label maker and I'm in heaven.

I began to look for God in the small things, because that seems to be where He shows up in the biggest ways.

Armed with a Sterilite container, I set to work. I cleared an entire shelf in our pantry for the cans and cans of formula, which I stacked two high. Christian's feeding tube required an assortment of bonus supplies, like extra syringes and replacement MIC-KEY buttons in case his came out and wasn't usable. This was actually terrifying to me, since the feeding tube hole can close quickly, similar to an ear piercing.

The IV pole for his feeding pump was nestled into the corner of his room. In case of a nighttime spit up, the sleep apnea machine sat on a table in our bedroom near the bassinet to alert us in case he started aspirating.

Our living room floor became filled with toys and baby items, but I didn't care. I loved seeing his things all over the house.

Our living room and dining room table quickly filled with piles of paperwork. One end held stacks of law books; the other held medical printouts, forms, and research regarding Christian's condition. Little did I know that the dining room table held the two elements that were the crux of God's purpose in my life.

I was beyond nervous about using the feeding tubes and all of the equipment, and strangely grateful for the classes they'd forced on me. We had a list as long as my arm of scheduled doctor appointments. Yet the joy I found in spending time with Christian on our own and finally being his mom in every sense trumped all the nervous butterflies and worries.

LETTING GOD USE MY IMPERFECTIONS

There are a few phrases I hear a lot yet strongly disagree with. Permit me to share:

1. "God only gives special children to special people."
   That's just not true. I've seen people who don't take care of their children with special needs.

2. "God gives special kids to strong parents."
   Nope. God didn't give me Christian because I was strong. I am terribly weak. It's *because* of Christian that I've become stronger with God's help.

3. "I couldn't handle it."
   Yes, you could. If your child needed you to do something, you would do it regardless of the time, energy, or cost.

4. "God does everything for a reason."
   That's like saying God gives children birth defects. Instead of blaming God, we can let Him use our imperfections.

I was about to let Him.

Christian was born toward the end of my first year of law school. With the semester breaks I was able to have a little more time juggling his appointments and therapies, but all too quickly the second year began.

To quit law school wasn't even an option until we found out the seriousness of Christian's condition. It weighed on me—the time it takes to prepare and study is extreme; to add caring for a child with special needs and working full-time is madness. I desperately wanted to make the right decision for our family, and God provided the strength and ultimately the peace my heart needed.

My second year began. One of the classes I took was Mental Health Law, which was a blessing because it opened my eyes to the world of law as applied to disability. I was living this life, yet I had no idea the rights that were afforded to us. I knew there must be thousands of other families who needed help too.

Besides the extra work and sensitivity needed to care for Christian properly, there were mounds of hard-to-understand forms to fill out for insurance, therapies, social security, and all the other things he needed. It was beyond overwhelming and ridiculous. I'd reached out to an attorney whose retainer alone was beyond our means.

As I sat at the wooden table, poring over my textbook, everything came together. My passion for law became the gateway to help other families handle the intensity of the documentation and navigate their own journey. A renewed vigor coursed inside of me, but I knew something had to give.

The phrase "survival of the fittest" isn't quite an accurate way to describe life. In my case it was "survival of the stubbornest." I prefer to think of it as tenacity.

I was determined to be the best mom possible for Christian. His needs always came first, even over studying for law school. I scheduled every appointment, drove to every therapy and doctor's visit (most an hour-and-a-half drive each way), and applied for every benefit we could get for him.

When Christian was born, I decreased my hours at work because of his therapies and appointments. I wanted to stay home with Christian more than anything. His feeding tube automatically qualified him to have a nurse, an expense covered by insurance, but it was a double-edged sword. I was watching other people's sweet little ones during the day while someone else was watching mine.

It became a sore spot in my heart and yet softened me as well. I now understood the sacrifice every parent makes when they drop their kids off at day care. I prayed for God's help. On paper we had a way to make it work, but the Social Security office wasn't cooperating.

FINALLY, A BREAKTHROUGH

We had a difficult time getting approved for disability benefits. Christian's blindness automatically qualified him as disabled for purposes of Social Security insurance eligibility. Even though we met the remaining requirements, it felt like someone sat behind a desk all day with a rubber stamp, pounding big red "declined" ink spots over every application.

After about a year of swimming in Social Security paperwork, I went to our local office. When they called me up to the window, I carried Christian with me. The woman's face registered shock. She was not good at hiding it. I handed her my latest rejection letter, along with papers that "proved" he was blind. At the time I was still learning to be direct with people, but the frustration took over.

"He doesn't have eyeballs," I said.

Classy.

I surprised myself at the brashness of my statement, but I had no idea how we would survive if they denied us again. Christian's medical expenses were piling up, and to take Christian to his myriad of doctor appointments and therapies, I'd already cut my hours at work to part-time. This was our last option, and we were desperate enough to take it.

The woman looked from me to Christian, blinked a few times, then looked me straight in the eye. "I'll get this taken care of for you," she said.

Moments later we left the office, approved.

The sunshine felt warmer on my face. The birds chirped louder. We were now able to get Christian enrolled with the state's insurance program for children with disabilities and the Social Security benefits would cover what I'd been making.

I tried to take care of myself as well. I'm not sure how much sleep I got, but I made sure that we were eating properly, and I tried to go to church as often as I could. Somewhere along the way, though, I started to hit a wall. I couldn't keep up at this pace.

I was doing everything I could to keep my head above water, but it often felt like I was drowning. My friendships started to suffer because I literally didn't have time to do anything, and it was extremely difficult going places when I was carrying my baby plus ten extra pounds of medical equipment.

My friends were encouraging, "You're so strong, Lacey. How do you do it?" Yet I wasn't strong at all. I wanted to throw in the towel. *That's it, coach, I'm done. Take the weight off my shoulders.*

On the brink of collapse I held fast to the promises of the Bible. If you look around my house, you'll see the index cards I made during that time. Written in different colored ink are Bible verses stashed everywhere. It seems that when I need a certain verse, I'll open a random drawer and *poof!* There's a card with the exact words God needed me to see.

We are made perfect in our weakness.[1] It is truly Christ in us who does the extraordinary. It's God's strength that people noticed in me. I surely wasn't doing anything spectacular, just what had to be done.

I needed help, but honestly I didn't even know what to ask for. Our bills were piling up with all the work I'd missed to be with Christian during his surgeries and recoveries. The stress became too much. We were struggling in our marriage. Finances were more than tight. Chris was withdrawn and I felt alone. Our cycle of life became get knocked down, get back up. Rinse and repeat. I prayed for relief, and God answered in the form of a car show.

TEAM CHRISTIAN BLOCK PARTY

While God dealt with my weakness issues, He stirred compassion and creativity in our friends. I didn't even know how to ask anyone for help, but the beautiful thing about true friends is that they show up when you need them the most.

We had just scheduled Christian's second surgery. To help offset the medical expenses, our friends put their heads together and decided to hold a car show as a fund-raiser for our family.

The town of Woodbury came to life. The city granted permission for us to reserve the entire town square *for the whole day*! Local businesses got in on the action, and several donated 100 percent of the concessions and sound equipment. My friends even created Team Christian T-shirts to sell.

As word spread, a few bands volunteered to play at the event for free. The generosity of spirit was incredible as the community rallied behind our little family. They truly thought of everything—pizzas, clowns, a silent auction, praise teams. Our friend Pamela Randolph brought her RV to shield Christian in the event of rain. And what a blessing indeed, for it rained twice throughout the day.

I'd felt so alone, and yet hundreds of strangers wore our shirts and reached into their pockets to help our family. They shared stories from their heart about their own experiences.

The news stations got wind of the event. Channel 4 and Fox 17 News featured the block party, which foreshadowed the media frenzy headed our way.

God reminded me of His love for us in big ways that day. As fiercely as I love my children, I know God's unconditional love for us is more than I can fathom. The car show funds relieved an enormous financial weight and provided breathing room in our budget.

The love of our friends and family combined with the generosity of the people of Woodbury brought sunshine into a bleak situation. They were the calm in the eye of the storm.

The tempest was upon us, but we sought shelter in the safety of God's arms.

Chapter Six

A LONG STRETCH
OF NIGHT

*But wells don't come without first begging to see the wells;
wells don't come without first splitting open hard earth,
cracking back the lids. There's no seeing God face-to-face
without first the ripping.*
—Ann Voskamp, *One Thousand Gifts*

CHRISTIAN HAS UNDERGONE so many surgeries that we have operation *traditions*. Surgery is frightening, especially to a small child who can't see what causes the strange noises and sensations. It is always our mission to impress upon Christian that he's a superhero for being brave. He's going to be OK. He's Super-Christian.

Tradition number one: on surgery days he gets to wear his special Superman cape while Chris and I, along with our friends and family, wear our Team Christian shirts. In solidarity we face the worrisome hours ahead.

Our second tradition revolves around ribbons. My routine during the surgeries is always the same. I sit in the standard uncomfortable chair, stare off into the distance, and absentmindedly rub my fingers over the fabric heap in my lap. This bundle is Christian's prayer ribbon, a collection of cloth sent to us by friends, family, and Facebook followers.

Before his surgeries I log in to our official Facebook page and request people to pray over our little boy, for the surgeons to be rested and alert, for their hands to repair my baby, and for God's healing mercy. In addition I invite the community to send in a six- to twelve-inch piece of ribbon with a prayer written on it. We link them together into a long chain. We bring it to every surgery as a tangible reminder of the prayers being offered to God on our behalf.

The cool thing about the prayer ribbon is the creativity. One of my friends sewed fringe, bells, and bows onto a strip. Other people have used buttons or puff paint, and one person sent in a furry ribbon. Before Christian is taken back to the pre-operating area, we cuddle him and run his fingers over the material.

We tell him about the people praying for him, that he is loved and special. He's Super-Christian, and our God is a super Father who will keep him safe.

After the nurses take Christian from us, I clutch the ribbon pile and reread the Sharpie prayers and verses. The ribbons soak up my tears while I ask God to bless the beautiful people who are praying for our boy.

SURGERY #1

Surgery smells like Germ-X and fear. My faith stretched with every surgery because I was *forced* to let go. What happens is beyond my control, so I have to trust God with my child simply because there is no other choice.

The first obstacle Christian faced was how to eat. The cleft defect was so large that he couldn't even drink from a specially created bottle. As I mentioned previously, feeding specialists decided the best course of action was to insert a nasogastric tube (NG tube).

They snaked the slender tubing up his nose, down his throat, and into his stomach to feed him. Poor Christian must have felt like he was gagging all the time because they couldn't stop him from pulling it out.

The first surgery was relatively simple: replace the NG tube with a gastronomy tube (G tube). We weren't happy to have him go under anesthesia, but we were thankful for the G-tube solution, which would allow us to feed him through a much smaller tube directly into his stomach.

The whirlwind of the first few days after Christian's birth had taken a toll on us. The doctors explained what they were going to do and we nodded numbly.

Sign the papers. Sign our life away.

It was only because of our desperation for him to be able to eat without being miserable that we made it through. On February 22, 2011, we were escorted to the holding room before surgery. Christian was still in his incubator crib, the plastic walls a physical barrier between my precious little one and me. I wasn't allowed to hold him, but I could touch his tiny hand.

The nurses needed to sterilize him before surgery, so they'd removed everything but the warm blankets that snuggled him. This was the first time we'd seen Christian with only his IV, the rest of the tubes or bandages removed. It had been hard to grasp the magnitude of his birth defect, but now we could see exactly what had the specialists so concerned and puzzled.

I stroked his fingers and stayed with him until the last possible moment. I felt hollow when he was wheeled to the medical personnel only section.

As far as surgeries go, a G-tube insertion is fairly routine. Performing one on a four-day-old isn't.

The surgery went exactly as planned. Not only did the doctors insert the feeding tube, but they also closed a small opening in his skull where it hadn't fully formed.

The feeding tube was truly a blessing in disguise. Christian wouldn't stop pulling at the NG tube, but he left the G tube alone. In fact, he's super protective of it now. The insert is called a MIC-KEY button, and funnily enough, they upgraded him later to a mini-button.

MIC-KEY. Mini.

Mickey. Minnie.

Mouse.

Sigh. It's the little things.

Christian currently has an AMT MiniONE, which is smaller and has a lower profile so it doesn't stick out much, although after a few slides down the couch cushions, it has a tendency to pop out. His feeding tube has always been part of him, so he gets sad when we have to change it.

While the surgery went well, the recovery did not, and I experienced the frustration and panic of a mother who isn't being listened to.

WHEN NO ONE LISTENS

I don't have a medical degree. I'm not going to pretend that I know more than the doctors and nurses who were in charge of my son's care. However, I do believe that a mother knows her child and that it is the parents' right and responsibility to advocate for their baby. Unfortunately it took me awhile to grow into that role.

After the feeding tube surgery Christian was given a fentanyl IV drip. Looking back, I'm not sure why they gave a four-day-old something so strong. As far as I know, with the strength of fifty to one hundred times that of morphine,[1] it's not a standard pain medicine for this "routine" surgery.

G-tube surgery means a hole was cut into my baby's abdomen and stomach. That area would definitely be tender and painful, but forty-eight hours after the surgery they completely removed Christian from the IV, stopping all of his pain medication cold turkey. Why didn't they gradually wean him to a less intense pain medication? It would have been so simple to give him something else.

It made me sick to my stomach to watch my newborn baby scream and cry in pain for hours after his surgery, unable to sleep, unable to comprehend the pain he was feeling, and unable to see me or feel my arms around him. When I voiced my concerns, the nurses assured me that Christian wasn't in pain.

To put this in perspective, after recovering from a C-section, which, granted, is major surgery, I was given some heavy-duty drugs, then handed a prescription for painkillers for when I left, and was able to take over-the-counter medication as needed. Even much less invasive procedures allow pain meds for several days. Yet my four-day-old baby had his abdomen and stomach punctured, and he wasn't allowed anything to alleviate his discomfort.

I understand that many drugs can be harmful to infants, especially newborns, but finding a safe medication wasn't the issue. The problem was that *no one but me* thought he was in pain. He wailed and screamed for hours, unable to even cry himself to sleep, while I stood pathetically at his incubator, literally powerless. Even though I was his mother, I didn't get a vote or a say in the decision regarding pain management. So my baby cried and I wept.

NOT AN ADDICT

I begged them to give him something, but I was told, "No, he's not in pain. He's suffering from withdrawals."

Deer. In. Headlights.

It's true that babies can become addicted to pain medicine, and fentanyl is a strong drug, but I believed my child's cries weren't from addiction but pain! How does anyone expect a child to handle feeling nothing to suddenly feeling everything?

Despite my protests—*because what did I know?*—they gave him methadone, a drug given to addicts to stop withdrawal symptoms.[2] If Christian was, in fact, addicted to fentanyl, the methadone would help alleviate his discomfort.

I understood the justification behind their reasoning, but I disagreed with their assessment. The only time he wasn't screaming was when he slept. As soon as he awoke, he'd cry longer and louder. Every day I asked, "Are you *sure* he's addicted? Are you *positive* that withdrawal is the problem? Maybe he's just hurting."

"He's not hurting." They dismissed me with three words.

It would have been so simple to give him something for pain, even something with over-the-counter strength. Why wasn't it clear to anyone else that if a child is addicted to a drug that the antidote would relieve symptoms, not worsen them? Thus my child wasn't addicted.

Christian was inconsolable, and I was too weak to fight. I let them administer methadone for weeks before they finally released us. We should have been out of the NICU only a few days after that first surgery, but the hospital wouldn't discharge a patient "suffering from withdrawals," so our stay extended to a full twenty-eight days.

It was during these times that God strengthened my resolve, and I vowed to learn from my mistake of silence.

CLUB FOOT FIASCO

Along with the cleft palate and blindness, Christian was also born with a right *club foot*, which means simply that his foot grew in the wrong positions, so the tendons weren't as long as they should be. His little foot curved slightly inward, potentially causing mobility issues if left untreated. Part of correcting this meant we drove every week to get a new Ponseti[3] cast that would slowly stretch his foot into the correct position. The technician would stretch his foot a little and cast it. Then they'd pull a little more and recast.

On our third visit for casting, our orthopedist introduced us to a new doctor. After the new doctor cast Christian's foot, something looked off.

"Does this look right to you?" I asked the casting tech. She was a sweet, fun woman who'd been at our previous appointments, and I trusted her.

"Yes, why?" she asked.

"It looks painful, like it's not quite right," I said. Babies have flexible bones, and Christian cried every time they cast his foot, but something felt wrong to me. She assured me it looked great, so we left.

A couple of days later Christian's nurse brought him to me at work.

"I think his leg is broken," she said.

"I hope not."

She nodded. "I honestly think so. I gave him pain medicine and he stopped crying."

Please, God, no.

We took Christian back to the specialist and expressed our concerns. The kind doctor who set the cast was resolute that Ponseti casts cannot break bones. I was on one side of the exam table, and he was on the other with Christian in between.

"I need you to X-ray his leg," I said.

"I don't think that's necessary," he replied.

The old Lacey would have nodded and let them recast the leg, but I was not the old Lacey. God was building a work of confidence in me. I'd missed opportunities to stand up for my baby because I was afraid to be wrong.

I rose to my full height and leaned slightly over Christian's head.

"X-ray. His. Leg."

A few moments later the doctor walked back into the exam room holding Christian's x-ray film. He looked mortified.

Ever the professional, he clipped the X-ray to the light box and turned it on. "It appears," he said, "that there is a small chip near his knee." He used medical terminology, but all I remember is a wave of nausea. Christian had been in pain for a week, and I felt sick and shocked. I couldn't trust anyone to do the right thing for my baby.

I was Christian's only voice.

The weight of that realization left me feeling panicked and scared.

Thank You, God, that I followed my instincts.

"What do we do next?" I asked.

He looked sheepish. "Well, we put a cast on it."

Of course.

SURGERY #2

At the risk of sounding dramatic, Christian's second surgery almost killed him. The most important procedure for him had been inserting his feeding tube. The second most important was to close his cleft lip. The quicker this happens, the sooner the child can learn to form words and eat by mouth.

Our Super-Christian was three months old and about to undergo his first facial surgery. I was a wreck.

Everyone had reassured us and told me how strong I was, but instead of proving them right, I had one of those train-wreck moments that no one ever talks about. As soon as the nurses took Christian to the pre-operative room, I froze in the waiting area. Even though my own parents and friends were with us, wearing their Team Christian shirts, I felt desolate at that moment.

 Lacey Buchanan
May 23, 2011

I'm going to look back on this one day and ask myself how I ever did this. And I pray that I remember that it was by the grace of God and the prayers of so many people.

Instead of tapping into God's strength, I found myself vomiting in the family-sized restroom, tears and snot running down my face. This was not the Lacey I show on Facebook or the strong mom I had to be at his doctor appointments. My child's life—his future—was completely out of my hands for the next eight hours. Only God knew what would happen, and I broke down.

My three-month-old baby was under anesthesia for eight hours so the doctors could perform major reconstruction to his face. The plastic surgery required them to break the bridge of his nose, push the bones back, and sew together the sides of his face where the cleft had been.

When we got the call that surgery was over, a doctor escorted Chris and me to a small room while my parents and friends stayed in the waiting area.

"He did great. We were also able to stitch up part of his eyelid. You'll be pleased," he said. I squeezed Chris's hand, thrilled to pieces as the doctor reviewed the surgery details.

A few minutes later we walked back to the recovery room.

As I neared Christian's bed, I didn't recognize my son. Instantly I felt light-headed and nauseous. Darkness crept into my peripheral vision, and I wobbled. Chris grabbed for me, and I sank into him.

Blood poured out of the corners of Christian's eyes, soaking the gauze. Orange iodine coated his skin. His eyes were bruised, and his face was swollen to twice its normal size.

He was trying to cry, but he could barely open his lips from where they'd sutured his mouth. I felt like my baby was under a dark, pulsating red cloud of pain.

One hand flew to my mouth while my other arm remained firmly in Chris's grasp. I didn't trust my feet, didn't trust my voice, and definitely didn't trust the words "You'll be pleased."

I composed myself briefly and called my mom, who'd asked for an immediate update once we'd seen him. She answered on the first ring. My voice shook.

"It doesn't even look like him."

I wished I could take his pain from him. I would have gladly done anything to ease his suffering. "Please, God, transfer it to me," I prayed. "I can handle it."

The entire recovery process was a nightmare, but it was this surgery that changed everything for me. God pours us broken into His refining fire to mold us, and I was more than ready for

Him to douse the flames. I didn't know how much more I could take or how much worse things could get. Through the course of that night God tested my resolve.

THE MASK

I walked beside Christian's metal crib, holding his little hand as he was transferred to the intensive care unit. Each bump of his bed caused this terrible moan to leave his lips. It sent shivers down my spine; I've never heard anything like it again. The orderly settled Christian's crib into his room, and the nurses secured the IV and tubes running from his body.

My family had gone home, including Chris. I numbly watched them process my baby until one of the nurses came into the room holding a plastic oxygen mask.

I stepped forward.

"What are you going to do with that?"

She flexed the stretchy band connected to the nose and mouthpiece with one hand.

"We have to keep the area moist so it can heal."

"They broke his nose; he can't have that on his face," I said, taking a step toward her. She'd already made it to the top of the incubator.

She paused for a moment and looked me square in the eye. "Doctor's orders." She stretched it around his head, but it slipped. The mask popped onto Christian's freshly stitched face and his scream pierced my ears.

"Take it off!" I roared like a lion shaking his mane over his dominion.

Startled, the nurse removed the mask and huffed past me. I couldn't pick him up, so I pulled a chair up to his incubator and sang Third Day's "Just to Be With You," the song I still sing to him when he's sick or recovering.

The nurse came back in.

"You can't have that chair there."

I stared at her.

"In case of an emergency we have to be able to get to him. We don't have time to move the chair."

I pushed the chair toward the wall with my foot and turned my back. Another nurse joined her. In place of the mask they built a plastic humidifier around my boy. Thus I spent a long night on my feet next to Christian's side, singing and praying while he cried.

PAIN ISSUES AGAIN

I'll never understand why Christian's pain wasn't managed effectively. It wasn't until two years later after a third surgery that I realized this hospital's staff skipped the crucial morphine part of Christian's pain management and went straight to hydrocodone. When I saw the night-and-day difference between the way he recovered when he was given morphine in the first twenty-four hours after his surgery and then was switched to hydrocodone, it all clicked.

Yet again this surgery was another instance of my ignorance. I didn't sleep that night and can attest with certainty that Christian didn't either. His cries bounced off the small walls of his room.

When we hit hour two, I asked about pain medicine. Four hours in I begged the nurse to give him something else for the pain. Alas, no orders were put through. No medicine came, and Christian screamed through the night, the pain too much for him to even exhaust himself from crying. I prayed all night, standing next to his bed, hardly conscious of my sore feet and tired legs.

Later the next morning Christian's body had had enough. Without warning, the alarms blared. He was still screaming, and with horror I watched his blood pressure readings jump to

230/180 then spike at 300/250. That couldn't be right—numbers that high could kill an adult. Yet they had inserted a PICC line (peripherally inserted central catheter) in his foot, a delicate procedure that produces accurate readings on blood pressure. I ran for the nurse.

"His blood pressure is in the 200s," I managed to spit out. She looked at me.

"What?"

I repeated myself, and she ran out from behind the nurse's station to his room. She stared at the monitors, repeating, "That can't be right; that can't be right," as she bent over Christian.

I made my way to the other side of his incubator and pleaded, "You've got to get him some pain medicine."

She nodded and rushed out to request a doctor's order.

I stood over my baby, afraid at any minute he would stop breathing. How much could his little heart handle? How much pain could he stand before he lost consciousness? If my baby was going to die, he wasn't going to die alone.

I cried out to God. "If You work all things together for good, how is this good?[4] If Your plans for me are hope and a future,[5] what kind of future is this, always praying my child won't die?" It was the most traumatic experience of my life.

As I sang and whispered soothing reassurances, he continued to cry, but the numbers began to drop on the machine. The nurse returned after a short while and inserted morphine into his IV. And for the first time since he'd woken up from surgery about twelve hours earlier, my baby slept.

I kept vigilant watch over him, physically about to fall over myself. But I praise the Lord for granting me temporary nerves of steel that kept my eyes on Christian's chest and my hand in his as I anticipated he would slip away from me at any moment.

I listened to the monitors as he slept. The steady beeps assured me his heart was beating, but I was terrified the beeps would stop. This was only our second surgery, with countless more to come. How would we survive this?

We stayed in the hospital for five days before being released. Christian left with physical scars. I left with emotional ones.

CHOOSING TO TRUST

Since that surgery we've had five more. Three were simple ear tube placements, but the last two surgeries were big and dangerous.

A popular song called "Oceans" by Hillsong United ministered to me in unexpected ways. When I find my hands shaking or my pulse racing, I repeat the lyrics in my mind and pray them in my heart.

Some people can stand in the face of adversity and proclaim that God is faithful. And He is. But I'm quieter about it. I don't think it's my job to say what He's going to do, but I do feel like it's my job to say, "No matter what You do, God, I'm going to trust You."

He doesn't always give us the outcomes we want, because if He did, Christian wouldn't have been born with a birth defect. We prayed specifically that God would miraculously heal what the doctors had seen on the ultrasound.

I wanted Christian to be healed, but God said no.

Our circumstances looked like God's promises weren't being fulfilled, which brought me to this crossroads regarding Christian…do I trust God and His promises in the Bible, or do I not?

God gave me the grace to make this decision on my own. I didn't feel His anger or pressure, just a gentle nudge for God to reteach me what His promises *are*, not what I *thought* they were. With the exception of that afternoon on my lunch break where God pitched the "Blessings" song at me, everything I've learned has happened over small processes…a verse here, a circumstance there.

But God's ways are not my ways.[6] He sees the entire picture and I don't. My church's recent Facebook status reminded me that we view life through the spectrum of our personal hurts, wants, and desires instead of through God's lens: to ultimately have everyone come to know Him through Jesus Christ. I don't believe God *caused* Christian to be blind, but I believe that He will work out our difficult circumstances in such a way that gives Him glory.

Chris and I certainly asked God the *why* questions. *Why is this happening to us? Why are You punishing us? Can Your promises really be true when circumstances look like this?* I don't think it was wrong for us to feel this way. God certainly knew how we were feeling, so we cried out to Him with the questions that pierced our souls.

We wrestled with God, and He allowed us the space and grace to ask and mourn.

Interestingly God didn't answer us right away with a no-doubt-about-it thundering boom of a reply. Instead, over the course to time, patiently and lovingly, He continued to show us that He can be trusted and our circumstances have no bearing on the depth and truth of His promises.

God wasn't punishing us. In fact, He loved us so much that even our doubts about our situation weren't enough to separate us from His love.[7] Our heavenly Father cares about our heartache; it just takes time and practice to hold on to those promises when you feel like you're drowning.

I remember a specific instance when I was still working after Christian was born. My heart was in turmoil that day. When we took the kids outside to play, I sat at the picnic table and prayed for peace. I felt like I was walking on quicksand, and I was afraid to take the wrong step—make the wrong decision. Literally in that moment as I prayed for peace, a dove flew down from a tree and landed three feet from me. It paced for a few minutes then flew off. I'll never forget that small moment where I *undeniably* knew that God cared about my pain and that He was comforting me.

His truth is a firm foundation where we can plant our stubborn feet and cling to His promises. I wish I'd held on tighter during this time, but I promise that nothing shakes me from His grasp now. Even during the hard days when I feel like the rudeness and incompetence of others is enough to drive me to darkness, I tell my God and simply hold on.

"Not my will, Father, but Yours be done."[8] Amen.

Chapter Seven

SEARCHING FOR ANSWERS

Never be afraid to trust an unknown future to a known God.
—CORRIE TEN BOOM

A COUPLE OF WEEKS after Christian's major facial surgery I noticed one of the incisions on his skull looked infected. I finished his bath, wrapped him in a towel, and sat with him under the lamp to get a better look.

The skin was puffy and red.

Please, God, don't let an infection get near his brain. I notified Chris and dressed Christian in comfy pajamas, and we headed to the emergency room.

ERs on Saturday nights = no fun.

A staff member called us to an examining room at around 3:00 a.m. While the ER doctor didn't think it was an infection, he strongly suggested we follow up with our plastic surgeon. The next day I got in contact with our plastic surgeon, a new doctor to whom we had been referred because of her area of specialization. Dr. Sonya ordered a CT scan to eliminate any possibility of infection. We could take zero chances.

We waited. And waited. And waited for the results. When I was confident the results were available, I e-mailed the nurse and left messages. Finally a tired-sounding receptionist informed me that there wasn't an infection, but the doctor was concerned about Christian's skull and wanted us to come back.

I don't know how long we would have been waiting to set the follow-up appointment if we hadn't called.

A few weeks later we saw Dr. Sonya again. She told us that some of the plates in Christian's skull were closing too early, a rare condition called craniosynostosis (also referred to as craniostenosis). When this happens, the closing plates can cause brain damage and the skull will grow misshapen.

My baby has two completely unrelated and extremely rare birth defects? What are the odds?

Red flag.

Then Dr. Sonya explained how she would fix it. The "treatment" included an eight-hour neurosurgery where, as I understood it, they'd make an incision toward the front of Christian's head, slicing the skin open from ear-to-ear, pull up the scalp, and remove the top of the skull. Then they would shift the position of the skull and finally reattach the skull with permanent metal wires and screws.

Easy breezy.

I didn't say anything for a few minutes. The mental image of what she'd described was nauseating. It also didn't register.

The one positive feedback we always received at Christian's many doctor visits was that his head growth was beautiful, and we held fast to that one praise. The craniostenosis didn't make sense, especially since this type of diagnosis has to be researched by a neurologist. But one hadn't been consulted.

Dr. Sonya scheduled us for a follow-up appointment, and I got busy with research. Christian's pediatrician sent me a copy of his head measurements. Sure enough, they were all perfectly normal.

Another red flag.

Two months later we went back to the plastic surgeon. She looked at the old CT scan image, ran her fingers over Christian's head, and said, "We have to do the surgery. You can schedule it at the desk on the way out."

She didn't ask to see Christian's head growth chart. She didn't order a new CT scan to compare the sutures. She didn't seem happy when I said I wanted to wait before scheduling.

We needed a second opinion.

CRANIOFACIAL CLINICS

The days ahead seemed dark, but we know that God brings joy in the morning. After several depressing weeks, joy came in the form of the UT Medical Group's complimentary monthly craniofacial clinic in Memphis.

It was absolutely worth the three-and-a-half-hour drive Chris and I made. A panel of doctors reviewed our case, inspected Christian's medical records, pored over his CT scans and MRIs, asked tons of questions, and conducted an extensive physical exam. When they finished, all five specialists were in agreement.

One doctor acted as spokesman for the group. "I know and respect your plastic surgeon," he said, "but I disagree with the diagnosis of craniostenosis and would not suggest the surgery."

Relief flooded through me. My due diligence had paid off. I'd acted in Christian's best interests instead of agreeing to a doctor's whim. It was a proud moment, and I needed that win. I danced out of the office and immediately called my mom and dad with the good news.

LOVE IN ACTION

I'm thankful that God allowed us a break in between our grief. He showed us His care and love in big ways as well as small ones.

During this time I'd blogged about our troubles with our hospital. A woman named Julie Thomas reached out to me on Facebook. She introduced herself and mentioned that she'd been following our story. Her son was close to Christian's age and was also a NICU baby graduate. But her positive hospital experience was drastically different from ours.

We corresponded back and forth while we felt each other out. Julie was heartbroken over what we'd gone through and felt compelled to help. She lived near Nationwide Children's Hospital (NCH) in Columbus, Ohio, and offered to set up appointments, network on our behalf, arrange consultations, and get some answers. I found Chris in the living room and explained the plan.

"Are you sure about these people?" he asked.

"That's why you're going with me," I said. "If they're murderers, you can fight them while I run."

"Deal."

I started saving to cover extra expenses on the trip, but when Julie said, "I'll take care of everything," she meant it. She teamed up with her coworkers and threw a fund-raiser to get us there, opened her home so we'd save on hotel costs, and let us borrow her car to get to appointments. As if she hadn't done enough, Julie secured a foundation to match the funds raised. It was literally an offer I couldn't refuse. Before I knew it, Chris, Christian, and I were on a plane ride to Ohio.

Lacey Buchanan
August 26, 2012

Thank you so much for the donations that were collected to help fund our trip! Special thanks to our friends at inVentiv Health and the Ronald C. Cooper Memorial Fund! We are blessed!

When we landed, a welcoming committee waved "Christian's Crew" signs and cheered as we disembarked. I expected to spend the weekend awkwardly trying to not feel like an imposition, but Julie and her friends had other plans. They treated us like royalty. We drove to Bucca de Beppo and ate our fill, then spent a relaxing afternoon at the swimming pool. That evening Christian and Julie's son played on the floor while the adults chatted like old friends.

On Monday we visited NCH. When I walked through the doors, I was beyond impressed. Everything gleamed and the air smelled pure, clean, and rich. From the looks of the place they had the best of the best. Christian would have access to the latest medical equipment, and surely the doctors who worked there stayed current on the latest findings in their fields.

Christian deserved the best care possible, and I felt like NCH was the place to give it to him. While we sat in the waiting area, a brochure caught my eye. I pulled the pamphlet from the rack, and my breath caught in my throat. Since several doctors dismissed my concerns over two-month-old Christian's surgeries with "I don't know what you're worried about," the words leapt off the page and validated every fiber of my being.

No surgery is routine when it's your child.

Exactly.

GOING THE EXTRA MILE

I wasn't willing to skimp on Christian's care, so we pinched every penny and tightened our belts. While we were overjoyed with just the sheer possibility of having other surgeons look at Christian's case, our financial situation concerned me.

Even though I felt like the last few months had been a nightmare, God was working behind the scenes. To offset costs, Julie organized a fund-raiser that helped cover the expenses of our air travel and make up for Chris's unpaid time off. On top of that, we weren't charged for the medical consultations.

We were blessed to visit her office to express our gratitude for her coworkers' support and generosity. Even the workplace atmosphere reminded me of creativity and goodness. We walked into an artistic workspace. Instead of wall-to-wall cubicles like a call center, the stations were broken up, with a few cubicles in one corner and open tables along a wall. Everyone seemed to have a lot of personal space and freedom to decorate their area with pictures and special knick-knacks. The entire space felt inviting.

They'd already gone above and beyond with the fund-raiser, but Julie's company went the *extra* extra mile. Her coworkers escorted us to a long, narrow conference room with a projector at one end of the table and boxes of pizza at the other. As people took their lunch break, they came in, shook our hands, and grabbed sodas and slices of pepperoni and cheesy goodness. We had an amazing time.

DISCOVERING WHY

At this time we knew Christian's diagnosis was Tessier cleft palate, but we still didn't know *why*. My heart longed for answers. There was still a part of me that wondered if I had done anything wrong, if it was my fault.

Blame and guilt go hand in hand, and it was difficult not to cast that blame onto myself. In His infinite wisdom God said no to our prayers for a healthy baby. I was still working that out in my heart, but to have an answer to why—or even how—would help.

The two big appointments at NCH were: (1) meeting with a specialist who could perform some advanced genetic testing, and (2) seeing the neurologist for a third opinion about the craniosynostosis diagnosis.

Lacey Buchanan
May 12, 2011

Tomorrow is our appointment with genetics. This is what we've been waiting to hear since the day we found out about Christian's cleft. We will find out if this is genetic and if we will be able to have more children. Say a prayer for us!

Thankfully we didn't have to wait long for results. When we met with the geneticist, she gave us the reason Christian had been born with a birth defect. His condition was caused by amniotic band syndrome (ABS), which in some cases results in a cleft palate. Our ultrasound technician, Jennifer, had seen an amniotic sheet during the ultrasound, but the bands that attached to Christian's face had never been visible.

The guilt I'd carried was gone. There was nothing I did to cause the ABS. The best news was that ABS isn't hereditary. We felt completely relieved. Little did we know that baby Chandler would make an appearance within the next year.

Armed with this great news, we proceeded to the neurologist appointment. My insides were filled with anticipation and dread. I felt like this was the tie-breaker—the UT Medical Group said Christian didn't have craniosynostosis; Dr. Sonya said he did. So we'd agreed that we would follow whatever direction this doctor suggested.

Meeting with the neurologist showed us that not only do God's blessings come in big gestures (Julie Thomas!) but also as friendly faces. After the disdain we felt from our plastic surgeon, the joking, relatable neurologist was a breath of fresh air. He chatted about his kids, smiling the whole time, and put us completely at ease.

The best part was that he *listened*. He allowed me to talk about the diagnosis and show him the sutures in the CT scans. After a few minutes he asked what I did for a living. When I replied that I was a law student, he joked that he'd thought I was in medical school since I knew so much about Christian's condition. That confidence boost was exactly what I needed.

After our conversation the doctor took some time to review the charts, paperwork, and scans with us. We sat in silence, barely breathing. When he'd finished, he calmly and firmly gave us the news.

Christian did not have craniosynostosis.

That was it. After *several* "second opinions" from prestigious doctors we felt sure that Christian's skull growth was perfectly normal, and he didn't have a second rare birth defect.

Chris and I hugged each other fiercely. I closed my eyes and praised God that Christian would be spared the monstrosity of another operation. With the fear of the terrible surgery lifted from us like a gray fog, we looked ahead at the days to come with hope and gladness.

The next day we met with the Nationwide Children's craniofacial team. Groups of doctors walked in and out of our exam room, yet all day everyone smiled and gently interacted with Christian. The team treated Chris and me like the parents we are. Our opinions mattered, and they respected the information we were giving them.

The pressure of conflicting information weighs upon your spirit when your child's future is in someone else's hands. Constantly searching for answers and coming up short had been taking a toll.

In addition to taking us to Nationwide Children's Hospital, Julie took us to Shriners Children's Hospital in Cincinnati. Their team took their time examining Christian instead of merely running their fingers over his skull for ten seconds and glancing at an old CT scan. They came to the same conclusion as the doctors at Nationwide Children's Hospital: no craniosynostosis.

In the end, after consulting with a specialist from California, Nationwide Children's Hospital devised a plan to close the soft palate and repair Christian's lip in only two surgeries. It's amazing what happens when egos are checked at the door.

BACK TO THE HOSPITAL

Our prayers had been answered—at least God had spared Christian one huge ordeal. But Christian desperately needed his palate fixed, and insurance regulations required an in-state plastic surgeon. So when we got home, I scheduled a follow-up appointment with Dr. Sonya.

Since she always talked about how much Christian needed the operation, her current plan was to cut Christian's skull open. But after our consultation with UT Medical Group, I was ready for a new direction.

I felt strong. I'd gone the extra mile, done the research, and advocated for my baby. My demeanor was a far cry from how helpless I'd felt at the beginning.

When we got into the exam room, I shared the details of our trip. I told Dr. Sonya the panel in Memphis was willing to collaborate, to share their findings with our doctor so we could come up with a plan. This appointment was important, and I was excited to have us all on the same page. I expected that she would say, "Let me take into consideration their thoughts, and we'll get together and form a new plan of care."

Dr. Sonya isn't a rude person, but she is matter-of-fact. After I finished the explanations, I waited expectantly. She didn't ask to see the paperwork or for the names of the specialists we saw.

"I disagree," she said. "He needs the surgery."

The joy we'd felt after the panel's decision vanished, sputtered out like a limp balloon. Even though I was surprised at her answer, I squared my shoulders.

"Well, he's not having it."

The appointment ended abruptly, and we walked to the car deflated. I was beyond stunned that our surgeon so strongly disagreed with the findings of the teams in Memphis. How could she refuse to accept the second, third, and fourth opinions of the other specialists?

We'd prayed so hard, and it seemed like God had answered our prayer, but now we were back at square one with a doctor who refused to admit there might be a chance that she'd made a mistake. I knew I couldn't take Christian back to her. My maternal instincts were on high alert. I knew it was time to look for a new doctor.

For months I made myself sick over the decision, overanalyzing each part in my mind. We knew Christian had more surgeries to undergo, and we needed a new plastic surgeon.

INSURANCE WOES

Insurance companies were not our friends at this time. I made appointments with every qualified plastic surgeon in the state that had experience with cleft palate disorders. I drove Christian from one end of Tennessee to the other. Without fail the specialists took a look at our case and shook their heads.

"I'm sorry," they said. "Here's a referral."

Except the referrals were either out-of-state or to the doctor we no longer wanted treating Christian. Disappointment doesn't begin to cover what Chris and I felt.

We loved Nationwide Children's Hospital. The staff was as kind and good to us as they could be. The surgeon answered all of our questions and asked many questions himself to get to know us and Christian. We got to see firsthand his skill and expertise in handling Christian's case.

As I fought with the insurance company, our hope waned. So I did what any law student would do. I took them to court.

On October 5, 2013, I stood in front of a judge at the final appeal hearing with Christian's insurance company. This was our last shot. Christian's insurance company was represented by counsel, but all we had was my plea.

Eight days later we received our answer in the mail. The judge sided with the insurance company, so we got a big fat no. We were disheartened, disappointed, and unsure where to go next.

 Lacey Buchanan
October 6, 2012

Just got this letter in the mail today from Christian's insurance company. They have denied covering his surgeries at Nationwide Children's Hospital in Columbus, Ohio. This is what I expected. However, I know this is where God is placing us, so please be in prayer that the financial aspect of this will work out! With God nothing is impossible!

THE GIFT OF NO

I knew Nationwide was the hospital for us, but God doesn't always give us what we want. Instead He makes us wait for what we need.

Julie Thomas opened the door to some amazing experiences. Christian's case would have taken months and months longer if she hadn't answered God's call on her heart to reach out to total strangers.

In fact, this insurance denial was the pivotal point. Unbeknownst to us, God stirred compassion in the heart of one of our Facebook followers who ended up leading us to the surgeon who became our hero.

Yet during this time of disappointment we resigned ourselves to God's sovereignty, knowing that while we may wish we walked a different path, He'll give us the stepping-stones needed to navigate the rising waters.

My faith strengthened as I trusted Him through the *nos* to lead us to the *yes*. Even though Nationwide couldn't give us the surgery, their staff gave us peace. Christian wasn't a lost cause. His condition wasn't unexplainable. For the first time Chris and I began to see this journey through eyes of hope.

For I know the plans I have for you," declares the Lord, "plans to prosper you and not to harm you, plans to give you hope and a future.

Jeremiah 29:11

Pre-K
Year 2
August
25th
2014
Woodbury Grammar

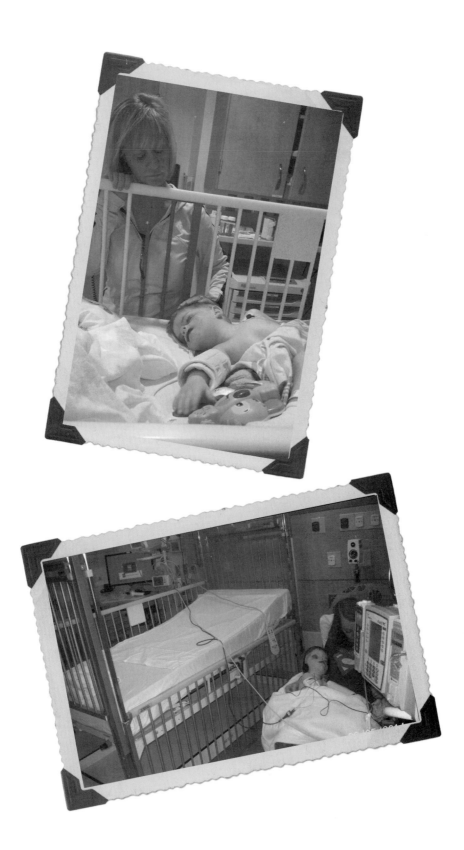

I am Five years old!

Kindergarten
Christian's First Day Of Kindergarten

I want to be a RADIO DJ when I grow up

Christian says this about Kindergarten: "Are you so excited? Is it the Blind School?"

August 8 Two Thousand Sixteen
→ → → → →

Tennessee School for the Blind

Ms. Ann Frensley's Class

Chapter Eight

PUBLIC OUTCRY

Sometimes God allows what He hates to accomplish
what He loves.
—JONI EARECKSON TADA, *THE GOD I LOVE*

A S MUCH AS I'd wanted to leave the NICU, it offered a
respite from a world that disapproves of anyone who
looks different. Now that we were home, I crept through
the public jungle, full of curiosity and nosiness.

We were ill-prepared for the pushiness, rudeness, and insensi-
tivity of strangers. Chris and I knew Christian looked different—
it would be ridiculous to ignore that fact—but what we were
absolutely not prepared for were people's loud whispers and bla-
tant stares. One man couldn't look away and smacked right into
a soda display.

It would have been amazing to have delivery service. The emotional toll of merely running into the grocery store to grab milk

pierced the veil of God's strength that I desperately clung to for survival.

At first I'd made the mistake of not shielding Christian from the whispers and stares. I quickly learned that to make each errand as effective and quick as possible, to drape a light blanket across the top of Christian's car seat after gently depositing it into the large shopping cart basket. Germs were a concern, as they are for most new mothers, and while he obviously didn't notice, I wasn't mentally or emotionally in a place to offer explanations to strangers.

Question-and-answer sessions doubled the time for each trip, so I covered him up, especially after his facial surgery when he was three months old. And still, going to the store became a dreaded chore.

When I see a blanket covering the top of a car seat, I assume the baby is sleeping. It never crosses my mind to ask the mother to see her baby. I simply smile and leave the mother alone to enjoy her few precious moments of quiet.

Not everyone shares this approach. It shocked me every time someone interrupted my produce selection to sneak a peek at Christian. And the same intrusive question always started the conversation.

"Oh, you have a baby?!"

No, that's my husband. He has Benjamin Button disease.

No, the car seat is my purse.

No, I'm practicing for motherhood with my cat. She scratches.

I'd smile, nod, and half-turn so they would get the hint to leave me alone. But alas, being inconspicuous was a pipe dream.

"Oh! Let me see!" And a hand would reach to remove the blanket.

"No!"

I wanted to rap every set of knuckles with a yardstick like a Catholic school nun.

They were always shocked, wide-eyed and mouths open. Their request was so innocent. What kind of mother doesn't show off her baby?

This social guilt led to rationalizing. *He has a birth defect. He looks different.* And he did. The fresh scars from his surgery to close his cleft lip were raised and pink, and the bruising around his eyes faded into a terrible yellow. His appearance was a far cry from people's natural expectations of what a baby looks like.

After one such incident I said, "Sorry, he's sleeping," and quickly pushed my cart away from a woman who wordlessly gaped after me. As I fast-tracked to the diaper aisle, God hit me with a thought so clear and bold, I stopped in the middle of the aisle.

Don't hide this baby.

THE WORST EXPERIENCE

One afternoon after a particularly long therapy appointment I stopped at a Walmart located in the heart of a college town. I grabbed what we needed and made it to the checkout without much trouble. However, I chose the wrong line.

As I waited for an eternity in mommy-seconds, a college kid in front of me became super-interested in my blanket-covered car seat.

"How old is your baby?" *Here we go again.* He asked the normal questions, and then the dreaded one. "Can I see him?"

"I feel like it's easier just to keep the blanket on him," I said.

"Oh no, it's fine..."

Really? And here we go playing twenty questions with strangers when all I want is a few minutes to myself to think.

I kept myself between him and Christian, not trusting him to keep his hands to himself. I didn't want him to pull up the corner of Christian's soft receiving blanket to take a look. But as the line inched forward, I needed to place my items on the conveyer belt.

I said it again. "No, he's resting."

"I'll just take a peek."

Why don't people understand the word *no*? I'll tell you why. It's not that they don't understand. They want to wear us down to the point where we'd rather give in than keep arguing.

Looking back, I see how God was using these situations to make me stronger, but at this point in time I was weak. After a couple more back-and-forths, and realizing that we were going to be in line longer than I wanted with no end in sight to the slow scanning up ahead, I acquiesced.

Do not hide this baby.

Since then I've answered so many questions about Christian that I have a small arsenal of responses in my belt. But on that day I was still learning how to deal with people. Just yanking the blanket off Christian was not the best way to go, so before I pulled back the blanket, I stressed to him that Christian didn't look like a typical baby.

"He has a birth defect."

I was met with a joke, "Is that even a baby under there?"

My stomach roiled.

"Again, you need to understand that he has a birth defect."

"OK, mama."

I slowly pulled the blanket back, and he gasped loudly, clasped his hand over his mouth, and literally jumped back away from us like he'd just witnessed a terrible car accident.

I almost burst into tears.

You know the scene in the movie *Sleeping Beauty* where Maleficent transforms from a woman into the terrifying dragon beast? Yup—my blood ran hot through my veins. I was instantly alert and powerful as my surprise at the overreaction morphed to incredulity, then anger. I'd never snapped at anyone before, but there's always a first. One day Christian will have to learn to stick up for himself, but this was not that day.

"Hey," I said, my back ramrod straight, my posture slightly forward as I drew myself to the cusp of my height and I faced him.

"This is my *son*. I *told you* he looked different. I didn't want you to see him, so thanks for making a painful experience hurt a little more."

He immediately began apologizing. "You're a great mom. He's gonna be fine."

I nodded and turned back to my sweet Christian, who was blissfully unaware that his mother grew up a little in that moment. I looked past his features and thought about who he was and what God had planned for him. Then I took a deep breath, covered him back up, and resumed emptying the shopping cart.

I managed to pay for my groceries, load Christian and the bags into our car, and get out of the parking lot on autopilot. On the way home I analyzed the scene, the kid's reaction, my words. That guy had made my day worse—like a maraschino on top of a sundae, though this cherry was rotten and the ice cream had melted.

So often we allow people to either hurt our feelings or push and prod us into a situation where we feel like our back is up against the wall. Then we "Christianize" our lack of self-respect by excusing the behavior and "turning the other cheek." Sometimes we need to not worry about appearing like a crazed mama bear and stand our ground.

Lacey Buchanan
December 15, 2015

Discrimination against people with disabilities is alive and well, guys. I know the truth and I am committed to sharing it until my last breath. Christian's life is worth living. He is not miserable. He is not suffering. He is joyous and filled with life and madly loved. His birth defect is NOT a measure of his value and worth. Period.

EDUCATING THE WORLD

The Buchanan motto: Educate the World! When the doctors laid out the plan for Christian's surgeries and therapies, Chris and I had big decisions to make. Each procedure has about a dozen steps. Some include months of preparation before the actual surgery can happen. So not only do Chris and I battle people's reactions to Christian's appearance, but we also fight criticism on how we manage his care.

For example, the procedure we get asked about the most is if we plan to "fix Christian's eyes." Yes, we will, but not right away. While that particular surgery is on the medical totem pole to-do list, there are others that trump it. Once Christian's cleft palate issues are completely fixed, the only disability he'll deal with is his blindness.

To create a more natural eyelid will take months of prep, and even then Christian won't have fully functioning eyelids. For there to be enough skin to graft, one plan is to make an incision behind each ear and insert a medical "balloon" into the area behind his cheeks. Every so often the balloons will be filled with saline to stretch the skin. After a few months the balloons will be deflated and removed. The extra skin will be used for Christian's lips and eyes.

That's pretty intense. And that's one of the simpler surgeries.

Months of preparation take away from Christian's quality of life, and I want his memories of childhood to be happy and fun, not a long string of surgeries and recoveries.

My sweet grandmother lived to be 103 years old. Toward the end of her life she'd pat my hand and remind me, "Now, Lacey. When I die, you make sure Christian gets my eyes so he can see." Right now the technology doesn't exist for those types of transplants, but I believe that one day children in Christian's situation will be able to literally see the world through someone else's eyes.

Until that day comes, Chris and I shifted the way we approached Christian's disability. While yes, the tissue around his eyes will be repaired, cosmetic procedures aren't as crucial as medically necessary ones. If we were to jump that surgery to the front of the line, Christian's feeding and speech therapies would be stalled simply to help strangers feel more comfortable around my son.

As we weighed our options, Chris and I came to the same conclusion: Christian didn't do anything wrong by being born with a birth defect. The *world* is wrong for assuming that he should have been aborted or that he has a terrible quality of life. He shouldn't have to suffer for their erroneous thinking. So why don't we let Christian be who he is and educate everyone with whom we come into contact?

Let's change the world, baby.

ANSWERING THE QUESTIONS

It's heartbreaking that in a society as obsessed with diversity and political correctness as ours, so many adults are blatantly rude to a child who looks different. Thankfully those situations are becoming less common.

Chris and I welcome people's questions, and I don't get tired of constantly repeating myself. This is part of God's purpose for me as Christian's mother and advocate. When a child asks his mom, "Is he a zombie?," I'm prepared for the parent's lightning-fast response of, "I am *so* sorry."

It takes more than a six-year-old's honest question to bother me these days. In fact, I welcome it when parents allow me an opportunity to explain.

I drop to a knee or squat to get on the child's eye level and look for a common thread. "No, he's not a zombie. He's a regular little boy. I see you're wearing a Star Wars shirt. Christian loves Star Wars too."

Another reaction we're used to hearing is the apologetic preface to a question. "I'm so sorry to ask…" But allowing someone the grace and freedom to ask questions means we can educate one more person. When we do, the world is a little better place for Christian and everyone else dealing with a disability. So hey, ask away.

However, not all questions are worded with tact. Children are given a pass up to a certain age, as they can be brutally honest. Their questions to their parents usually include "What happened to his eyes?" or "Are his eyes bleeding?" or (and this one used to really hurt my heart) "What is *that*?"

Learning to deal with this was difficult, but it has toughened my skin. Those comments don't bother me anymore. I understand that people are simply curious about Christian and have good intentions. At his core Christian is a rough-and-tumble little boy who loves cars and trucks, being tickled, and playing with his brother.

The only reactions that bother me are when parents ignore teasing from their children or if someone is callous. However, it's futile to stay cooped inside just in case someone decides to be rude. We choose to embrace life and not worry about the comments. We know they'll come, but now we're prepared for them.

Worry Less

While Chris and I have learned not to worry what people say, or even *how* they say it, our friends have a harder time dealing with people's rudeness. I've grown used to the stares. It's natural for people to do a double-take when they see Christian. Our brains are wired to respond when something seems out of the ordinary, and Christian's appearance isn't typical.

One day while I was picking up snacks at Walmart with my friend Annie, a group of teenagers started whispering. Annie overheard them say, "Ugh, look at that baby."

I hadn't heard the comment, but her eyes filled with angry tears. I thought she might walk over and give them a piece of her mind.

Comments really bothered me for a long time, but as I explained to Annie, people's insensitive knee-jerk reactions to Christian aren't always right, but most of the time the strangers aren't actively trying to hurt our feelings.

I love her for the protectiveness she felt over Christian, and many of our friends are the same way when we go shopping or out to dinner.

It saddens me that bullying is almost a certainty for Christian's future. I'm thankful that he doesn't quite understand the words people say now, but there will be a time that he comprehends fully. My heart breaks for the day he comes home from school and tells me he's been picked on or teased. I've seen the damage that adults can do, but kids can be just as cruel.

There are so many things to be thankful for. Truly the happier moments outweigh the sad. There is so much laughter and joy in this little boy.

Lacey Buchanan
May 3, 2011

I look at Christian and I don't see a deformity. I see the baby boy I carried. I see my son! I'm beginning to think that other people are starting to see Christian for who he is: an amazing little boy.

But I won't ignore the sad moments—I'll listen to what they have to teach me. Each time people act rudely, I wish I could— *poof!*—make them disappear. The world doesn't need your negativity. It's not welcome.

There's a Dorothy Northwood song that says without rain clouds, we would never appreciate the sunshine. How true that is. Our sunshine is sweet indeed because we have seen the rain.

A REFLECTION OF GOD

When we choose to love others, despite their differences, we glorify God in His creation. Instead of hearing people say, "I'm sorry," as if Christian had died, I want to hear, "Congratulations! Christian is learning how to survive and thrive in this world."

God helped me shift my thinking. Instead of seeing curious strangers as the enemy, I became determined that I would show people that Christian was my baby, my child, and that God had created him just the way he was.

I realize there are other families going through the same thing, who are loving and raising their children who have special needs, kids who aren't *handicapped*, but different. I like to say that Christian is "differently abled"—he uses his other senses (touch, smell, sound) and vibrations to get around this world.

Christian isn't a typical kid. He isn't handicapped, just different.

Time allowed me the privilege of looking back at all these solitary moments when people were inexplicably drawn to him.

Even if they don't know or recognize Christian from Facebook, YouTube, or television, strangers flock to him. This is God's calling on Christian's life.

It's as if people sense something different and special when they get around Christian. They want to know more about him. I believe it is the Holy Spirit working through him. I can't explain the events that changed the course of our life any other way than this: Christian's life is a reflection of the God who created him, not a mistake to be hidden, but a masterpiece to be seen.

Chapter Nine

A COMMUNITY OF
SPECIAL KIDS

*The area where we struggle the most is often the area of
our greatest effectiveness.*
—MANDISA

THE MOMENT CHRISTIAN and I entered the lobby at Special Kids Therapy and Nursing Center, I was shocked…at the *non-reaction.*

No one gave us funny looks.

No one stared.

No one had questions about Christian's condition or asked what was wrong with him.

People in the waiting area naturally glanced at us when we walked in, but after a quick smile they went back to their books or phones.

Had we stumbled into an alternate universe?

The Special Kids Center has an incredible mission: to change lives for Jesus Christ. They serve children who simply need a little extra help, children who are medically fragile, and all sorts of diagnoses in between.[1] The staff lived up to their purpose statement. Everyone showed us the utmost respect. Without us saying anything, they seemed to understand that we were at our breaking point and went above and beyond to make sure we were comfortable.

After four months spent in the NICU, at doctor's appointments, and in operating rooms, the time had come to begin Christian's therapies. We had four therapy sessions per week, each lasting between thirty minutes to an hour. Christian and I both learned a great deal, but the real test was carrying over the lesson into daily life. Kids take in so much through incidental learning during the first five years of their lives from activities as simple as watching *Sesame Street* or coloring.

With Christian I couldn't point to a sign and say, "That's the letter 'A'" or "This car is blue." I can't describe pictures to him the way I can with his brother, Chandler. If I tell Christian that we're looking at a picture of a zebra, he doesn't know what I mean.

I knew therapy was extremely important for Christian, so I squeezed time into our day to practice what we learned each week. However, it never felt like I worked enough with him at home. Mommy-guilt is an unwelcome guest, and I felt the weight of not doing enough or not doing things *well* enough.

There were moments when the day had been so crazy that I was tempted to skip Christian's therapy practice so I could study. Getting my law degree meant new opportunities for our family and ultimately more financial room. But then I'd look at my baby who couldn't make these decisions for himself. If I didn't practice with him, he didn't practice. He was completely at my mercy to help him get better. In an instant the decision was easy. My kids would always take priority over school. The books stayed closed for an hour longer, Christian grew stronger, and I stayed up later.

A Gift of Time

Special Kids became an integral part of our lives. When you're driving over four times a week for four different therapies, it's crucial that the people you work with are truly invested and care about your family. It's a bonus when the teachers fall in love with your child.

When we met the therapists, they treated Christian like any *normal* kid would be treated. The experience shook me. Instead of people avoiding us, not including us, or always having a negative comment or a sad remark, the therapists were cheerful. Every time we walked in, they greeted Christian like they'd been waiting all day for his arrival.

It was the Special Kids staff who shifted my perspective about raising a child with a disability. I knew I was ill-equipped to give Christian what he needed; I simply hadn't been trained. But what I could do is make sure we never missed an appointment, take copious notes, and practice with Christian every chance I got.

Unfortunately adding in extra time to practice with Christian meant less study time and absolutely no "mommy needs a break" time. After a few months of practically killing myself with our schedule, God showed love to us through our friend Amanda Parks.

Thursdays were our craziest day. I left work early to get Christian to the last therapy appointment offered for the day, driving half an hour to get to Special Kids. This meant another half-hour commute back to the house. Chris didn't get out of work until seven o'clock, but my class started at six-thirty. Thankfully my mom offered to watch Christian until Chris got home.

After kissing Christian good-bye, I jumped back in the car for another hour-and-a-half drive through rush hour to Nashville for class. I barely made it on time each week.

Lacey Buchanan
February 27, 2013

I log our medical mileage every month for tax purposes. Generally we run between 400 and 450 miles a month. For February, we have logged almost 750. No wonder I'm exhausted!

When school was over for the night, I prayed for clear roadways so I could get home in an hour. This crazy cycle ended once Amanda realized what was going on.

She lived close to Chris's job and sweetly volunteered to watch Christian until Chris got off of work. This was an incredible blessing. After therapy I dropped Christian off at her house to play, and Chris swung by after work to take him home. By doing this, Amanda saved me hours of travel time because Woodbury is in the opposite direction of my law school.

This also formed a precious bond between Christian and Amanda. She played with him, rocked him, and snuggled him. My little boy loves hearing Amanda's voice. Her gift of time allowed me some much-needed breathing room, and the stress she relieved can never be repaid. I thank God for her generosity of spirit and sometime will repay the favor.

WORRYING LESS

I'd finally met a group of people who understood what it was like to live every day with a child who needed special attention and care, and who probably also felt alienated. While I had to mentally prepare before going to the grocery store, I was able to relax and enjoy Christian at Special Kids. I didn't have to worry about someone saying something stupid or insensitive, and I didn't have to worry about losing my cool. Finding a community who understood what we were going through made me feel like turning around before we left to give the famous three-finger *Hunger Games* Katniss salute to the waiting room.

Having the opportunity to have experts work with Christian, especially having the same teachers over and over, made such a big difference for us. Every parent worries about their kids—it's natural and instinctual—but we worried that Christian would never be able to take care of himself as an adult.

Lacey Buchanan
December 15, 2015

Things Christian thanked God for during our prayer tonight without any prompting: home, Hope and Ashlynn (his nurses), playing with toys, Special Kids, Minions, playing games, Ms. Katherine and Ms. Karen (his therapists), couch. Mostly in that order! This is a perfect depiction of my Christian! What a sweet and goofy little boy I have!

Organizations like Special Kids do so much more than give peace of mind to parents; they literally change the course of these kids' lives and offer hope. We'd been told in the NICU that Christian would need extensive therapy, so I started researching different centers. A friend told me about the quality of work and compassion of the staff at Special Kids. It was truly an answer to prayer.

The staff and therapists showed us a love of Christ each time we visited. Beyond their daily kindness, the policy at Special Kids is to never turn away a family if insurance doesn't cover the full cost of treatment. They value children over money, and the community supports this by participating in fund-raisers.

We still worry about Christian's development, and continue to monitor it, but we're not experts in childhood development and rely heavily on what we learn from the doctors and therapists. Having this unique set of support alleviated so many worries and concerns.

PHYSICAL THERAPIES

Christian had a few different therapies, but one of my favorites was physical therapy. These specialists taught Christian the different developmental milestones and gross motor skills that a typically developing baby does on his or her own, such as sitting up, crawling, pulling up to a standing position, and walking.

Christian had rolled over by himself and reached for toys with my help (big wins). I would dangle toys near his hands and coax him to grab them. Once he mastered that, I moved the toy a tiny bit farther away, allowing him to broaden his range of reach. Eventually this led to Christian learning to search for items by stretching out his arms and feeling with his fingers.

We were proud of those accomplishments, but his development had stalled there. He needed to learn to hold his head up, to sit up, and eventually to pull himself to a standing position. These small accomplishments are so easily taken for granted, but at Special Kids the tiniest of achievements are rewarded and praised.

Before we could teach Christian to push himself into a sitting position, he first had to learn head control. Neck strengthening is a result of the famous "tummy time." Walk into any baby section of a store, and you'll see toys and colorful mats of every shape, size, and texture designed to help babies get their heads off the ground. Some of these mats have water pockets and noisemakers to motivate the infant.

Unfortunately these toys don't work for blind children. Babies learn to turn their heads or lift and hold them so they can see objects around them. Christian didn't have that motivation, so we had to find other ways to encourage him to hold his head up.

Since he had no incentive, Christian simply lay on the floor and rested his head on the carpet.

We needed him to learn that holding his head up was a positive thing. To achieve this, the therapist positioned him at the top of an angled pillow, his head at the peak, belly on the mat, and feet on the floor. At first he rested his chin on the mat, until he heard a rattling sound.

The therapist sat cross-legged a couple of feet in front of Christian and shook a toy.

Shake, shake.

Then a different noisemaker.

Rattle, rattle.

Squeak, squeak.

The noise signaled that there was something in front of him, something fun by the sound of it. He instinctively reached toward the sound, inadvertently lifting his head. We cheered, and Christian's face lit up.

He'd rest his head again, and instantly the noise returned. He stretched his little arm out, again lifting his head. We clapped and praised him. Eventually he could lie on his tummy on the floor with the toy placed out of his reach. He quickly caught on that we loved his head being off the ground, and he grinned as we applauded for him every time.

 Lacey Buchanan
December 20, 2011

So proud of Christian for an awesome day at therapy! He did really good, worked hard, improving every day!

Slowly but surely Special Kids taught him to sit on his own and eventually stand up. It took a while for him to learn how to walk. I can't imagine how scary it must have been to take that first step in a dark world, but he trusted me and his therapists enough to toddle toward us.

Watching Christian learn to walk taught me a lot about taking steps of faith in darkness when I can't see where God is directing me. My son trusts me to lead him safely even though he can't see where each step will take him. In the same way, how much more will my Father lead me where I need to go? God promises to lead the blind by ways they have not known and to make dark places light.

I don't have to have all the answers.

I don't have to know what God is doing.

All I have to do is take God's hands and let Him guide me, just as Christian holds my fingers as I guide him safely.

The biggest lesson I've learned is that I don't have to see in order to trust Him. I only need to walk.

Christian graduated out of physical therapy when he was two and a half years old so he could begin to learn skills specific for blind children. He was ready to begin vision-related services, such as learning to use a cane, sighted guide travel, and safe mobility practices. Special Kids isn't a center that focuses 100 percent on the needs of the sight-impaired, so his physical therapy ended and we continued with his other classes.

I've learned that I don't have to see in order to trust Him. I only need to walk.

OCCUPATIONAL THERAPY

Along with gross motor skills, Christian needed help with fine motor and life skills. When he was little, Christian's hands were always pulled up to his chest, like in a prayer position. All the time. It was adorable, but we needed him to feel comfortable with the space around him.

Christian also wouldn't cross his right hand over the left plane of the body. He always used his right hand to touch his right foot, never reaching across to the other side. The therapists explained that since he had no reason to cross his arm, he just didn't. Makes sense, but we had to work through getting him comfortable enough to do so.

Occupational therapy was super-critical. One of our goals for Christian is to teach him to be as self-sufficient as possible. Minor tasks like taking off socks took weeks of appointments, but we were so proud when he was able to remove them by himself.

To develop fine motor skills, the therapists used a lot of puzzles with textures and random shapes. They placed them in Christian's hands and helped him use his fingers to feel the boundaries of each piece. Then he would feel the puzzle board, trying to find the right void that matched the puzzle piece. Christian loved this game and quickly learned to identify which pieces needed to go in which slots.

His therapist also used sorting toys, lacing beads, and shape sorters to develop Christian's fine motor skills. This type of therapy later translates into things like turning doorknobs, tying shoes, opening and closing containers—all day-to-day activities that any adult will need to be able to do.

Some other activities that would prepare Christian for adulthood were learning how to manipulate Play-Doh, properly hold and use a crayon, turn pages in a book without skipping any, and stack blocks without knocking them over. We use these skills dozens, if not hundreds, of times each day—typing on our computer keyboards, texting on our phones, turning on the car radio or a faucet, getting dressed, slicing vegetables for dinner, or opening a bottle of water.

Christian wasn't able to perform even the simplest of tasks that most kids learn over time because he couldn't watch someone do it. There were so few opportunities for him to practice unless Chris and I purposefully scheduled time. If we were rushing out the door to get to our appointments for the day, oftentimes I didn't have an extra ten or fifteen minutes to allow Christian to practice dressing himself. As his skills become more complex, they require more time to practice, so we've learned to work practice time into our daily routine.

SPEECH THERAPY

Speech therapy will be part of Christian's life for a long time due to the severity of his cleft. Not only are we working to help Christian develop the speech skills he struggles with because of his vision impairment, but we're also dealing with the issues that his cleft lip and palate cause and how it affects his speech. The combination of the two disabilities makes this even more difficult.

For example, my son Chandler knows when I'm cooking because he sees me standing at the stove with a spoon in my hand. I can say "I'm cooking," and there is an instant understanding of that phrase. But if I am doing the exact same thing and tell Christian, "I'm cooking," it has zero meaning to him. He can't see me standing at the stove or see the spoon in my hand.

I have to physically hand him the spoon, let him feel the ingredients in the pan (before it gets hot, obviously), and show him how to use the spoon to stir. Then I let him feel and taste the food once it's done, not that he will agree to taste it though. We have to spend about thirty minutes walking Christian through every single step of an activity for him to comprehend something that a sighted person understands with a two-second glance.

This is one reason I say Christian is so smart. Not only does learning involve numerous steps, but also he understands and masters the skill, even with all the extra that it takes.

Children learn language two ways: listening and watching the context of how and when we say things. In fact, it's an indicator that your child might not be able to hear well if he or she is constantly watching your lips when you are speaking to them.

Additionally Christian's therapist taught us to put his hands on our mouths while we spoke so he could feel how we shaped the words. Now that he's older, we're telling him, "Christian, put your tongue on the roof of your mouth."

For him to get comfortable with that was a big win. Because of the severity of the cleft palate Christian still uses a feeding tube and probably will for a long time. Thus he's not used to having food or anything in his mouth. This is why feeding therapy is crucial for him and other children with adversities to oral stimuli.

The second part of Christian's speech therapy is teaching Christian how to communicate effectively. He doesn't understand speech at an age-appropriate level. This causes a lot of frustration on his part because while he knows exactly what he wants or what he's trying to say, he doesn't always know how to tell us.

This is a struggle, because even though we can figure out what he wants (eventually) from the context of what's happening at the moment, it doesn't help Christian's speech progress. It also doesn't help his behavior. We don't want him to learn that screaming and crying are appropriate methods of getting his way, but at such a young age there is only so much he could comprehend.

Now that he is older, we say, "Christian, please stop screaming. If you want a blanket, you need to say, 'May I have a blanket, please?'" When he complies, he is immediately rewarded for his manners and proper speech by getting what he asked for.

FEEDING THERAPY

Feeding therapy is a constant battle. Some days it feels like we're winning, but this is an area in which we can quickly regress. Every win here is a big win. For example, Christian still can't chew food, but for a while we got him to let these food puffs called "melts" sit on his tongue.

However, that didn't last long.

We run into the same problem that many tube-fed kids deal with. They subconsciously decide that since they are getting food through their tubes, they don't need it in their mouths. Christian has no connection between feeling full and the experience of savoring, chewing, and swallowing. From his point of view there's no reason to eat a banana, because the satisfaction of eating comes from the tube.

We take for granted that infants instinctively know how to suckle when they are born. From there, eating skills develop from drinking liquid to eating purees, then soft, mashable foods, then solids, and so on.

Christian didn't follow that pattern because he's used his feeding tube since he was four days old. When I went through feeding tube training, no one explained that it was not only safe to continue feeding him by mouth, but also that it was crucial to do so. Unfortunately my ignorance resulted in our battle of immense proportions: an extreme oral aversion coupled with a child who is sensory defensive.

I wish mealtimes were as simple as, "When he's hungry, he'll eat."

Many people ask if Christian will always be reliant on his feeding tube. My answer is always the same. "I hope not."

The fact is, physically and mechanically, Christian *can* eat by mouth at this point. However, mentally speaking, it terrifies him.

He does not understand why he should put food in his mouth. He's not alone in this situation. It can take years of therapy and even intensive feeding clinics to get tube-fed kids to eat by mouth once they don't medically need the feeding tube any longer.

At this point in his journey there is nothing medically stopping Christian from chewing and swallowing food. However, since he couldn't do it as a baby and toddler, he's still rejecting the entire idea. I believe he would literally starve to death before he agreed to eat.

Even though we have a long way to go, feeding therapy has helped a lot with his oral aversion; he will momentarily put a piece of banana on his tongue before spitting it out. After Christian had the surgery to repair the cleft, he started drinking from a sippy cup.

This therapy has taught us patience. The harder we push, the more frightening it becomes for him. We've learned that the developments have to come at Christian's pace. There has to be the right balance of scooting him past his comfort zone without halting the progress by pushing too hard.

After Christian's two palate surgeries his development levels grew so quickly. He did in one year what a typical child would attain in two years. He's made amazing progress to catch up, but we still have a long way to go.

ELMO TO THE RESCUE

Christian is a repeater. Without any visual cues, he heard only how we asked him questions.

"Do you want a blanket?"

If he wanted the blanket, instead of saying yes, he'd mimic the request. "Do you want a blanket?" If he didn't want the blanket, he would ignore you.

I thought it was cute at first, but this wasn't a long-term solution. This is where Elmo became our best fuzzy friend.

Christian loves *Sesame Street*, so I'd find "Elmo's Pizza Box Dance" on YouTube, and he would listen intently. When it was over, I asked, "Christian, do you want to hear it again?"

His answer: "Do you want to hear it again?"

Instead of hitting the play button, I said, "Christian, say yes or no." We knew he understood those two words, and I was pretty confident he understood how to use them.

This was a wearisome part of our therapy homework. Christian knew we knew he wanted to watch the show again. He'd repeated the question, hadn't he? That had always worked before.

I hated seeing him upset and frustrated. We've had to allow him to experience disappointment and anger because, in the end, it is for his benefit.

He had to learn to say yes and no at the appropriate times, so we worked and worked on it, using Elmo as our incentive. Eventually it clicked for Christian that saying yes meant Elmo got to play again, and he happily said yes, yes, yes automatically every time the episode ended.

GOD'S FINGERPRINTS

We see God's fingerprints all over the Special Kids community, from donors to patients to therapists and the entire team. We saw God in the small wins with Christian's development, and we saw Him through the people He'd installed in our lives before we ever knew Christian would need their indirect support.

God will always be our ever-present help in times of trouble,[2] but I believe He expects us to do our part too. At the beginning of our journey I had to gather enough courage to speak up for what we needed. I also had to let go of pride and accept help when it was offered. Oftentimes it was saying yes to other people's kindness that allowed God to provide the best solution.

My boss never had qualms when I needed time off from work. While I desperately wanted to quit my job and stay at home with Christian full-time, it wasn't possible until Christian was eighteen months old. God blessed us by allowing me to go part-time at work, but we wouldn't be able to make it on Chris's salary alone. We saw God's blessing every time my boss waved me out the door to take Christian to his therapies.

We also saw God's blessings during the annual Special Kids race.

No family is turned away at Special Kids, but most insurances don't pay for a full year of therapy. This means a hefty chunk of change comes out of the parents' pockets. To alleviate the financial burden, Special Kids hosts a one-mile, 5K, and 15K run.

It's a wonderful day of camaraderie. Local businesses set out booths, donate swag, and show their support for the heroes at Special Kids.

Our family and friends wear their Team Christian T-shirts and a few of us run in the race together. This past year I ran the 15K, and as I came up to the final stretch, I veered to the sidelines where my Australian friend Cassandra held Christian. I scooped him into my arms and ran with him to the end.

The best part of the day, however, is when all the little patients line up for the Fun Run. The announcer counts down, and the crack of a small firing pistol signals the beginning of the race.

Christian sits in the stroller, and Chris takes off. I run beside them, cheering for Christian. When we get close to the finish line, Chris unstraps him from the stroller, and we hold his hands so he can walk across.

The year I was pregnant with Chandler, Christian had just turned two years old. He still wasn't walking alone, but he could walk if we held his hands. So when we approached the finish line, Chris and I got on either side of Christian, and each took one of his hands.

We planned to triumphantly walk across the finish line, hoping for an *a-may-zing* photo opportunity of this sweet moment. Christian made it right to the edge of the finish line then promptly planted his feet. He would not budge.

The crowd was cheering him on. *One more step! One more step!*

Chris and I gently tugged at him, trying to get his heels off the ground, but he refused. I laughed so hard that I could barely see. He is *such* a turkey!

Much to Christian's dismay, Chris finally picked him up and set him over the finish line. As soon as the kids cross the line, the volunteers place medals around their necks. After Christian received his, Chris lifted him onto his shoulders in victory.

Every time we attend one of the fund-raisers, my heart is overwhelmed with emotion. My little boy has a beautiful life ahead of him, and Special Kids deserves a lot of the credit. It's a sight worthy of the Olympic Games when this community cheers on the special kids that cross that finish line.

Chapter Ten

HATRED FROM BEHIND THE KEYBOARD

*When wealth is lost, nothing is lost; when health is lost,
something is lost; when character is lost, all is lost.*
—Billy Graham

I T STARTED OUT innocently enough. I posted a Facebook
status with a picture of a contented Christian after a meal.
The caption read: "He's gonna be a chunky monkey!" In reality
it's difficult to overfeed babies who eat from a feeding tube. It
was an off-handed update, one of the rare moments I felt like a
typical mom sharing snapshots of her day. I expected comments,
but not all of the well-intentioned advice.

"Add cereal to his formula."

"He'll get full if you mix in baby cereal."

"Instead of giving him so many bottles, just add rice to his
formula."

We weren't shy about Christian's medical updates, but I hadn't realized how many people didn't know that Christian used a feeding tube. I thought it was obvious he couldn't drink from a bottle, but I've learned the adage is true—never assume.

So when people left negative comments online about Christian's eating habits, I brushed it off as ignorance. They didn't realize he was using a feeding tube. No harm, no foul. There is an immense amount of work that goes on behind the scenes to feed Christian that folks simply don't see.

But one comment stuck out among all the rest. I knew this woman. She and I had been introduced at a social event.

Her comment read: "There's more to mothering than shoving a bottle in a baby's mouth."

Uhhhhh...

Her comment bothered me, yet people had said worse and I'd shrugged it off. Perhaps it's easier to dismiss negativity from a stranger. Maybe it bothered me so much because I knew her personally.

The angry side of me thought, "That's ridiculous. Everyone knows there is more to mothering than shoving a bottle in a baby's mouth." It was such an ignorant statement.

Then the wistful side of me jumped in: I wish I could give Christian a bottle when he cried, or nurse him when he was upset. But we had to teach him to self-soothe without nursing or bottle-feeding.

Then the defensive side came out. I was running myself ragged making sure that Christian's every need was met, that he had access to the best available therapists and doctors. After all that we'd been through, how could someone insinuate that I lazily did anything I could to keep him quiet instead of taking care of his needs?

To be so poignantly criticized was wrong.

It hurt.

It was also the last straw.

Two clicks of the mouse and she was deleted from my friends' list.

Don't need that drama. Bye, Felicia.

TIME TO EAT

Apart from a specialist, you'll never find someone who knows more about a certain illness or disease than the parent of child who is sick or has special needs. I absorb every piece of literature, medical journal, or online information I get my hands on, and I ask extensive questions at each doctor's and therapy appointment. The doctors worked with us carefully on Christian's nutritional needs, giving us basically a crash course in proper nutrition.

Feeding tubes have actually become a blessing, but I found the lugging of equipment and exact measuring overwhelming when Christian was little. Bottle-fed babies will suck for comfort, but when a child with a tube gets overfed, he vomits.

When Christian was an infant, we pumped breast milk, and later gave him formula, through his feeding tube. When he was old enough for his system to handle solids, we pureed lean proteins, fruit, and veggies just as many parents do. Except Christian received his meals by stomach instead of mouth.

Now that he's a little older, I admit that I love being able to feed him healthy foods without a fuss. I don't know too many little ones who will eat kale and salmon, but because Christian doesn't taste his food, it's easy to ensure he gets the right amount of fruit, vegetables, lean protein, vitamins, and minerals every day.

This is not the case with our second son, Chandler, who has an affinity for bland foods and sweets.

Chicken nuggets? Yes.

Broccoli? No way.

THE WORST OF ALL

When people have nothing better to do with their time, they troll the Internet. They look for ways to be divisive because they're unhappy with something in their own lives that they don't understand how to deal with.

We've had our share of nasty comments, but the worst was when people implied that we should have aborted Christian. The first time someone suggested that we were selfish for giving him life, I felt stunned.

Punched in the gut.

I should have *aborted* my baby because he had a disability?

I'd grown accustomed to people laughing or making fun, but this opened my eyes to a new evil. There were people who looked at my child and thought, "You should be dead."

My sweet, innocent Christian had to grow up in a world where people believed he should be six feet underground because his life wasn't worth anything.

Dead.

Because he was blind.

Because he didn't look like everyone else.

I clicked the laptop shut and sat in silence.

I couldn't give Chris or my parents one more heartache, so the words festered in my spirit like an inferno deep in my soul. Just like in Jeremiah 20:9, there was a fire shut up in my bones that I couldn't ignore, but I had no idea what to do.

To retort or retaliate was counterproductive to our goal. I wanted people to feel like we were open to their questions. Even some of our friends will still apologize for accidentally saying "Christian, look at this!" or "Look at me." It's a natural thing to say, and I wish they didn't have to be so careful about each word. It's OK to mess up, and I try my best to give grace.

Little did I know that my eventual response would be the catalyst that sparked the greatest change in our lives.

Lacey Buchanan
March 27, 2011

One day, when Christian is old enough, I will be able to stand in front of him and say "I loved you too much then to give up on you. I love you too much now to give up on you. You are an amazing person who God chose to be my son and I am SO thankful for you." How sad it would be if instead I'd had to explain to him in heaven why I killed him before he ever had a chance to be loved.

DEFINING WORTH

Our society's definition of worth is messed up. Since when is someone's personal worth measured by how much he contributes to our economy? If that's the case, there are a lot of people in this country who would be deemed worthless. Thank God, literally, that He doesn't look at us through those eyes.

I started a new Bible study, and the verse of the day was 1 Samuel 16:7, "Man looks on the outward appearance, but the LORD looks on the heart" (MEV). King David was an undesirable in his society—the youngest brother and a shepherd. That was two strikes against him in his world, but God uses the "least of these"[1] and makes them great.

There are still countries where parents drop off their babies at an orphanage if they're born with a disability. Sorry, baby, you can't live with us. Buh-bye.

In South Korea, for example, it is common practice for mothers to leave their babies with disabilities helpless in the streets.

Abandoned.

Defenseless.

Exposed.

This infanticide broke the heart of a man named Lee Jong-rak. He built the "Baby Box," a drop-off location for mothers who don't want their infants because they aren't perfect.[2] Together he and his wife raise these beautiful children.

"They're not the unnecessary ones in this world," he says. "God sent them here for a purpose."[3]

Yet Americans have the same preconceived notion: that it's more rational to abort a baby with disabilities rather than let him live. It's horrifying, yet I recently saw survey poll results on Facebook that showed the majority of people believe the life of an unborn child infected with the Zika virus should end in a post-viability abortion. Similarly the abortion rate for babies diagnosed with Down syndrome in utero is astronomical.[4]

We still have a big battle to fight if it's 2017 and we think it's OK to kill a baby who might have a disability. How many perfectly healthy children are aborted who were misdiagnosed? And how many babies with a disability were killed who could have had an amazing life? A tiny part of me sort of understands how people think it's compassionate, but I firmly believe that a disability doesn't determine quality of life.

Lacey Buchanan
March 27, 2011

Since when is a cleft palate and being blind crippling? I know one thing: we have all seen that ignorance really is a crippling disability.

My husband is a perfect example. He was a completely healthy baby with no medical conditions as a child, yet he had a worse quality of life than Christian does. His childhood was full of pain and isolation.

They're not the unnecessary ones in this world. God sent them here for a purpose.

Even as advanced as we think we are, the world's perception of what is *great* is backward too, which can be expected from a world that doesn't follow God. People have actually looked at us with pity, "Oh, poor thing. He won't get married."

Really? How do you know? Blind people get married.

Even if Christian chooses not to marry, the Bible says that marriage isn't for everyone. If he stays single, he's not worth any less than anybody else. Does marriageability determine our worth?

Christian is physically blind, but the greater tragedy is the world's spiritual blindness. If I had to choose between never knowing God and never seeing a sunset, it's an easy choice for me. One of those is so much worse than the other.

God gave me a verse for each one of Christian's surgeries. Each one was specific and special in its own way, perfect for the time. For Christian's palate surgery, the verse was Isaiah 42:16, "I will lead the blind…I will turn the darkness into light" (NIV).

I was blind when Christian was born. I was angry with God, asking Him what I had done wrong and telling Him that He was cruel. People are blinded by their pain, their childhood, but I believe 100 percent that it is worse to be spiritually blind than physically blind, and yet all people could see when they looked at Christian was his lack of eyes.

It shook me to read the words that girl wrote to me—that she thought them and that she had the nerve to send them to me.

Inexcusable.

But God used the words meant to destroy and created something so beautiful, so much bigger than I ever thought possible. I became more active on my Facebook page. It felt like I was on a mission to show the world that Christian's life wasn't worthless. His quality of life was awesome: he was well fed, clean, had plenty of toys, and his parents adored him. He was safe and happy.

Just like when God admonished me for covering Christian's car seat with a blanket to run errands, I felt His voice again. I wouldn't hide this baby.

INTERNET TROLLS

About this time I started blogging more often. Writing became a therapy, a great way to vent and let go of the feelings I kept locked inside. It wasn't healthy for me to hold on to hurt, and since each doctor's appointment could bring a new onset of bad news, I had to release it.

I also became more open on my Facebook page with details of our journey. Ninety-nine percent of the people were kind and encouraging, but the vulnerability exposed us to the darkness in people's hearts.

Social media is a great place to say things that you'd never say to someone's face. This is what cyber bullies do: troll the online seas like pirates searching for victims, and in the absence of anything else to occupy their time, they pounce on anyone they see as an easy attack.

We were accused of Photoshop-editing Christian's face to get sympathy and using his disability to selfishly raise money for our own pleasures. Someone who makes fun of a child with a birth defect is a pretty low human being, but God reminds me that the war is not against flesh and blood.

I completely empathize with the parents who lost their son at Disney and the parents of the child who fell into the gorilla cage in the spring of 2016. The public outcry against the parents was horrendous, and frankly it's no one's right to threaten someone when disaster strikes. Where is the sympathy? Where is the kindness? Those parents lived through horrifying nightmares, and as a society we did our best to make their lives miserable.

I understand because these trolls came after us.

"If I see that kid on the street, I'll murder him."

"Kill that thing with fire."

"Don't leave your house or I'll rape you."

Those were the tame ones. We received comments that included a group of people discussing how they would perform sex acts to pictures of Christian. The worst comments were so vile and evil that they terrified me to the core. We immediately reported them to the FBI Cyber Crimes Unit, and they instantly followed through.

The majority of these comments would never be spoken face-to-face. How many people would walk up to the mother who lost her child to an alligator attack and say out loud that she deserved to lose her baby?

It breaks my heart. Some days I loathe to check the comments because I know there will be hateful or rude statements. And they hurt.

One time when Christian was two months old, a stranger made some particularly rude comments. I cried on the way home from the store. When we got inside the house, I wrapped Christian in a fuzzy blanket and cuddled him while I told him how perfect he was and how much he meant to me.

While I want to retaliate after hearing a mean remark or after reading someone's ugly response to one of my posts, the only thing I can do is be an example of what God calls us to be. Lord, have mercy, I don't always get it right.

OPENING BLIND EYES

We don't know what's going to happen for Christian. God may never allow Christian to have physical sight, even with all the advancements in technology today. We just don't know. But through Christian and his story God has given many people spiritual sight because of how He's used him. That includes me.

I can see how God is using Christian's disability. His disability isn't that bad, but with Christian there is a bit of a shock factor because he doesn't look like anyone else. If I say, "My child is blind," people expect to see a typical-looking child who may have his eyes closed or special glasses on. They aren't expecting a little boy whose eye tissues never formed and doesn't have eyelids.

Christian doesn't look like a "blind child," so people assume there are much more serious issues at play, like mental impairment. However, while Christian has some developmental delays, he's extremely smart and excels in certain areas.

Christian is a typical boy in so many ways, just like any other kid his age. He loves life, loves to play the piano, tells jokes, takes karate, and had an amazing first week at kindergarten.

There is so much joy watching your kid play sports and learn skills. With Christian I feel that joy is magnified when I watch him practice with karate. His sensei is amazing and looks for ways to be a better teacher to him.

He pulled me aside one day and said, "This is how I would normally teach a kid to do this move. Help me figure out a way to teach Christian." I demonstrated how we guide Christian's arms and hands when he's learning a new skill.

Christian is a typical boy in so many ways, just like any other kid his age.

His sensei adopted a more hands-on approach. I would help Christian keep his balance while the instructor moved Christian's legs and arms through the proper motions. After a few practice moves Christian performed successfully on his own.

#ProudMamaMoments

I can't imagine missing out on these moments just because a doctor might say, "He'll have a poor quality of life." And while no doctor ever said that to us, the grave predictions we heard before he was born do not in any way match up with his reality.

One of the things Chris and I had to learn was not to worry about what life will be like for Christian when he is older. We can only do what we can today to prepare him and try to make this world a better place for him.

We make decisions now that will pay off for him in the future, but to worry about what his condition will be like in ten years doesn't help us, and it certainly doesn't help him. This mind-set shouldn't be confused with long-term planning. God says to plan, but He also tells us not to worry, so we try to do one and eliminate the other. For example, Chris and I set realistic expectations based on Christian's vision impairment and work accordingly to get him the care he needs. We don't sit and dwell on the activities or events that Christian won't be able to participate in because he can't see.

Even though people have come to know God's love through Christian's story, I can't honestly say, "It was all worth it." God knows I would give Christian sight if it in were my power to do so, but I see beauty through the ashes, wonder through the hardship. God is fulfilling a promise, leading the blind by ways they have not known. We always think of physical blindness when we read the word *blind* in the Bible, but spiritual blindness leads to an eternity without God.

If Christian never gets physical sight, the first thing he'll ever see is the beautiful face of Jesus—and hopefully me next! Christian has taught me so much and given me more perspective than I could have learned in a thousand lifetimes without him, and he's only five years old. What God has done in this short amount of time astounds me. I can't wait to see what the years ahead have in store for him.

Chapter Eleven

THE VIRAL VIDEO

Sometimes it's the words we choose not to say that speak
most loudly about our character.
—LYSA TERKEURST

NAMED THE "WORLD'S ugliest woman," Olivia "Lizzie" Vasquez spent her entire life being bullied. She, like Christian, suffers from an extremely rare disease. In her case there are only three documented cases in the world. Her disorder doesn't have a name, but it caused an inability to gain weight and blindness in one eye.[1]

I was on my lunch break at work when I saw a video about Lizzie on my Facebook newsfeed. I clicked the play button, and God opened the floodgates.

Lizzie mesmerized me.

She didn't know she was the world's ugliest woman until she saw a video someone created with pictures of her. People's comments mirrored the hatred we'd received: do the world a favor and die.

In many ways Christian and I were just scratching the cyberbully surface, yet here she was, a survivor.

A victor.

Lizzie learned to stand up for herself. She produced an award-winning documentary called *A Brave Heart: The Lizzie Velasquez Story* and gave a speech at the prestigious TED Talk at TEDxWomen.[2] She used her disability as a platform and through the years gave a voice to the voiceless, the beaten, the misunderstood. Lizzie Velasquez is my hero.

Almost a year had passed since that mean woman had messaged me on Facebook. I still hadn't shared her opinion that Christian should have been aborted with anyone. It dug a deep place in my soul and rooted in my heart. I couldn't bring myself to say it aloud.

Apparently nap time at the day care center where I worked was God's special time to talk to me. I pulled out my phone and watched Lizzie cover her face with the flash cards that shared her experience growing up with her condition. Her message resonated. I knew what it felt like to be different because the stares and comments about Christian were directed at me. Hurting my son destroyed my heart worse than anything someone could ever say to me personally.

As I sat spellbound watching the video, I thought about Christian's reality. I knew the world was a better place *with* him. But how many people looked at him and thought the world would be a better place without him? The fire in my bones raged, and I knew what had to be done.

I never wanted Christian to hear someone say that he was the ugliest person in the world. Instead of hiding my baby to protect him, I had to show him to the world to strengthen him.

Lacey Buchanan
May 8, 2013

Sometimes I wonder how someone can see a picture of Christian with a huge smile on his face and a shirt that says, "It's cool being me," and still say things like "poor baby." I'm thankful for the compassion that they have toward my C, but poor, he is not. I guess I struggle to see the pity in any child with special needs, but especially in my spoiled rotten, loved by thousands, living-the-life little guy.

I grabbed notebook paper off the shelf, found a pair of scissors, and shuffled through a bin of unsharpened and broken crayons for a marker that hadn't dried out. I cut the paper into quarters and started writing our story. No edits. No second guesses.

When I finished, I had a small paper-clipped stack of lined, wide-ruled sheets in my purse. I couldn't wait to get home.

THE VIDEO

My one-year-old was napping when I walked in our door. I chatted briefly with his nurse, checked on my baby, and set up the computer in my office.

I'd never done anything like this before. I didn't even have a YouTube channel. The extent of my social media savvy included Facebook and MySpace (remember that?).

Christian stirred slightly when I gently lifted him out of his crib, but he nestled into my arms and fell back asleep. I wanted to make sure that Christian was able to lie still for the whole thing, so I kept his soft blue blanket wrapped around him and made sure his special pacifier was within arm's reach.

After a practice run-through I restarted the music on my computer and hit record on my phone. As "Give Me Jesus" played, Christian rested on my shoulder, his dark blond hair slightly tousled from his nap. One by one I held up the individual cards to the screen. Each slip of paper held only a few words:

When I was fifteen, I met Chris and we fell in love, it started. I shared a picture of us on our wedding day.

When I was twenty-three, we found out that we were going to have a baby.

We were so happy.

At my eighteen-week ultrasound we found out we were having a BOY!!!

We were even MORE excited.

Christian stirred and lay back into the crook of my arm. I held up my favorite pregnancy picture. I wore a long-sleeved button-down blouse with the bottom part open to expose my belly. A blue Christmas bow rested jauntily on the bump.

We named him Christian. ☺

A week later we got a phone call. Something was wrong with Christian.

We were crushed.

As Christian grew, doctors became more and more unsure.

What was wrong? Would he live? Would he be mentally impaired?

The smile I'd had when I showed the pregnancy picture vanished. The pain of the memory still fresh.

On February 18, 2011, Chris and I went to the hospital to deliver Christian.

We didn't know if we would come home with Christian or not.

At 9:32 AM, Christian came into the world…screaming!

He was ALIVE!

My face broke out into a huge grin. I couldn't help but get emotional as I remembered hearing Christian's first cries.

But it wasn't that simple…

Christian's condition was much worse than we originally thought.

He was born with a Tessier cleft lip and palate. He couldn't even close his mouth.

The smiling girl on the computer screen vanished.

His condition is only one of fifty in the entire world.

But it got worse…

Christian's eyes were also clefted. They just didn't form. They just weren't there.

Our baby boy was blind. We were heartbroken.

I sniffed, praying that I could get through the rest of my papers. Tears threatened to fall, but I mustered strength from somewhere deep inside. I squeezed Christian tighter and continued.

We didn't know what to do or how to raise a child who couldn't see.

Christian had surgery at four days old and stayed in the NICU for four weeks.

I showed a picture of Christian in his hospital bassinet. Monitors and equipment filled the background. I'm leaning over him with a proud new mama smile.

When we brought him home from the hospital, things were hard.

Anytime we took Christian out in public…

People would stare…

And whisper behind my back, "Look at that baby."

The music faded as the song ended. The only sound was the computer fan and the shuffle of papers as I reached for the next one on the stack.

Kids would ask their mom what was wrong with "that baby."

I couldn't go anywhere without someone doing something to point out Christian. After laying down that sheet, I pressed play on my computer. The next song's intro started, a lovely melody to fill the background of a hard story to tell.

Some people would even ask me, "What's wrong with your kid?"

One girl even told me I was a horrible person for not aborting Christian in utero.

Give me Jesus.

I was miserable.

But as Christian got older, he started laughing and playing.

A smile spread across my face as I showed a picture of Christian grinning after his three-month-old surgery scars had faded.

And when people would stare, Christian would start giggling...

And they would giggle too.

I held up a picture of Christian wearing his Super-Christian T-shirt, face to the sun, yellow and blue balloons adorning the background. His expression was full of life, full of joy.

People started finding me on Facebook...

Or recognizing Christian from hearing about him.

So we made a TON of new friends.

People started telling me how Christian inspired them.

And how beautiful he is.

And things got a little easier.

Christian is growing and healthy!

I couldn't stop smiling at this point. The music's tempo swelled and pulled my heart along with it.

Anyone who meets Christian falls in love with him pretty quickly.

Those judgmental glances and whispers don't really bother me anymore.

Because I know how beautiful Christian is.

Inside and out.

I also know that I did the right thing by not aborting Christian.

As the chorus of "How Great Is Our God" played, I showed a

photo from Christian's one-year-old photo shoot. We both wore white long-sleeved tops and jeans. I'm holding Christian up to my face, his hands on my cheeks as I give him a kiss.

He is the love of my life!

I held up another photo from that same session. Christian and I are both facing the camera, his blue scarf clutched in one little hand. I think he was licking it. The tissue around his eye is bright red, and his cleft is noticeable, but so is the grin on his face and the pride in his mama's smile.

And he is a miracle!

I also know that I did the right thing by not aborting Christian.

After a shot of Christian in his Superman tee, I moved the powder blue blanket Christian was wrapped in and proudly held my sleepy boy to the camera. I gave him a kiss on his cheek and turned off the camera.

When I finished, I sat in the chair holding my sweet baby, empowered.

GODTUBE

The video didn't create a lot of traction overnight. I hadn't expected it to, honestly. My plan for this video was simple. I wanted to create business cards with the link to the video so I could hand them out when people had questions about Christian. When I'm in line somewhere, there's never enough time to explain every-thing. This would simplify the process.

Besides, when I did take a few minutes to explain, the person's reaction was always the same: sad eyes and a well-meant, "I'm sorry." As bad as it may sound, I didn't want pity.

I posted the link to Facebook.

Friends shared it.

My family cried.

God stepped in.

Two days later I woke up with hundreds of notifications on my phone. GodTube.com featured the video on the homepage, and it had received twenty thousand hits. A few hours later the viral video was at forty thousand hits and growing.

I woke up in a reality so far different than what I'd become accustomed to.

The video took on a life of its own. *Huffington Post* got wind of our story and shared the video on Mother's Day. Christian's story trended at the number one spot.

NOT ALONE

A few days after the video went viral, I lay in my bed reading through some of the comments and well-wishes that people had left. By this time more than six million people had watched the video of Christian—watched me share my love and heartbreak for my little boy.

This level of response was out of the realm of anything I ever could have imagined. More than two hundred people left encouraging comments, thanking me for my bravery, for giving a voice to my baby, for risking even further criticism.

"You're a good mom. He's lucky to have you."

"I was feeling sorry for myself until I saw this video. Thanks for giving me perspective."

Lots of people shared that they were in similar situations; their child dealt with teasing and bullying because of a birth defect or some type of disability. A community naturally formed.

As I scrolled through comments, I realized that people were

linking to Christian Buchanan on Facebook. This seemed strange to me since my personal profile page had my name, not his.

I clicked on a link and realized that someone had set up a Facebook Fan Page for Christian. I couldn't believe it. The page had thirty-five thousand likes.

The response to the video didn't change Christian's diagnosis, but it showed me there were people in my corner. The worries over our finances and our marriage seemed less of a burden as one sweet person after another encouraged us. Each night when I went to bed, I opened the Facebook app and felt some of the day's struggles and weight lift from my shoulders. Here were hundreds of people cheering us on. I could be brave.

One night I lay in bed and responded to as many comments as possible. More than six million people watched me pour out my heart, and I was overwhelmed with the love they poured back to me. Fourteen months earlier I would never have dreamed my life would take me to this point. I'd been so wrapped up in our own problems that I didn't stop to think. I wasn't in this alone.

I love reading personal stories of how people were encouraged by our story. Some people chose to private message me instead of share their thoughts publicly. More than one young woman told me that if she was ever in the same situation, she was now going to choose life.

Those stories truly warm my heart, and I never tire of them. Somehow our story is their story too, and I'm strengthened by their solidarity.

God wove the threads of this story together long before Chris and I sat heartbroken and empty at an ultrasound appointment. God orchestrated this from the beginning, and I am in awe of what He has done. We didn't simply survive; He made us victorious in the face of hate.

People kept saying I was brave and special for sharing our story. The truth is, I wasn't special; I was just a girl who followed an idea that God whispered into her heart.

Chapter Twelve

GIFTS FROM STRANGERS

*If through a broken heart God can bring His purposes to
pass in the world, then thank Him for breaking your heart.*
—OSWALD CHAMBERS, *MY UTMOST FOR HIS HIGHEST*

O UR TRIP TO Ohio with Julie Thomas opened a whole
new world for us. I felt like we had a plan. The only
problem was that after the craniosynostosis misdiag-
nosis, we didn't have a plastic surgeon anymore. The goal was
clear: find a qualified surgeon to repair Christian's cleft palate
and close the roof of his mouth.

Night after night I fell asleep praying for God to perform
another "Julie miracle" and either bring the right people into our
path or let my search take us to the right people. After losing
the insurance battle, I wasn't sure I could handle another major
disappointment.

But while God is faithful, He doesn't always answer right away.

Weeks passed, and I was no closer to a solution. While we didn't have a definitive time frame, we knew the surgery needed to be done soon. After extensive research I drove up, down, and sideways across Tennessee to interview dozens of surgeons.

Unfortunately each visit ended the same way. They couldn't close the palate. Medically speaking, the gap was too wide.

I fervently believed that God had a way laid out for us, but that road was not clearly marked. Weeks turned into months, then salvation came in the form of Marisa Graham.

I hear people complain about social media, but God used the Internet to bring instrumental people into our lives. One day I came home to a cardboard package on our front steps. I hadn't ordered anything, so after settling Christian inside the house, I checked the return address and set the package on the table. Gingerly I cut the tape and opened the flaps. Inside were movie tickets, a restaurant gift card, and some baby toys. I opened the envelope taped to one of the toys and pulled out a note: "For the person who watches Christian so he can stay occupied during your date night."

Blown. Away.

How could one person be so thoughtful? Chris and I hadn't been on a date in years. The generosity renewed my tired spirit. I promptly sent a thank-you card, and a friendship was born.

After several e-mails and a few more surprise presents, Marisa pulled "the Julie card" and asked if we wanted to check out the craniofacial cleft palate clinic at Riley Hospital for Children in Indianapolis.

What were the odds that this could be happening to us again? I figured since Christian is a one-in-a-trajillion kid, that his road to recovery would follow the same odds. God, however, bestows countless blessings upon His children. After Chris and I talked a few times, we accepted Marisa's offer.

Marisa's creativity knew no bounds. She printed up spiral-bound booklets titled *Do Not Disturb—Super Hero at Work: Super C's Informational Packet* with pictures of Christian in his Superman cape and T-shirt on the cover. Inside was a screen shot of the ABC news compilation from the viral video, pictures of Chris and me with Christian, an entire page with the screenshot of my Facebook post the day our insurance company denied Christian's out-of-network surgery at Nationwide Children's Hospital, and the story of our quest to find a plastic surgeon who could handle a case as rare as Christian's.

Marisa took over the grunt work, meeting with specialists and CEOs at Riley to ensure we had appointments and consultations with various medical groups. The week before our visit she e-mailed me, "Don't bring diapers—I've got it all taken care of!"

I couldn't believe we were on another whirlwind experience. Chris's boss generously gave him time off. I felt like God was saying, "Buckle your seat belts. Here we go again!"

Our little family drove to Indianapolis for this next adventure, excited at what the future held. When we arrived at Marisa's house, we hugged and cried. After getting us settled, she sat Chris and me down on the sofa and shared her secret: Unbeknownst to us, she had taken a doctor to lunch before we'd arrived. Over salad greens and sparkling water she shared the obstacles we'd been facing with one of the surgeons we'd be meeting.

He agreed to help.

We spent the next few days at Riley meeting all the teams involved in a cleft surgery of Christian's proportion: anesthesia, registration, coordinators, and doctors. In the midst of the chaos I was able to shake the hand of the man who would fix my child.

Dr. Roberto Flores reviewed our case, performed an examination, asked us questions, and carefully listened to our concerns.

He took an interest in our boy that was missing from our previous doctor. Together we formed a new plan of action.

Stage one was to create the hard palate in the front closure, and then, six months later, stage two: close the soft palate in the back of his mouth. These surgeries were complex and dangerous because Christian's palate was so wide and the procedures included breathing and bleeding risks.

As we were getting ready to leave, Dr. Flores looked at me and said, "We're going to make sure we do everything we can for Christian."

There weren't fireworks. Angels didn't sing. But this was the moment when God proverbially set things in motion.

HITTING A WALL

A few days after we returned home, a representative from Riley let us know that while they tried to get pre-authorization from the insurance company for the surgery, they'd been met with a big fat *no*. Part of me knew better than to put too much stock in the insurance company. They'd denied our request to have the procedure done at Nationwide Children's Hospital in Ohio. As far as they were concerned, in-state surgeons could care for Christian. Despite a mass number of appeals explaining that those same surgeons had already turned us down, the company didn't budge.

 Lacey Buchanan
October 11, 2013

Reason number 276,958,421 that I hate insurance companies. Was just on the phone for 59 minutes and 36 seconds exactly, only to be transferred twice and then told I had called the wrong number.

One night before class I had a few rare extra minutes, so I went to the Rafferty's restaurant across the street from the school to grab a bite to eat. While I was waiting for my bill, my cell rang. The caller ID showed an Indiana number, so I answered.

When I heard Dr. Flores's voice greet me, I couldn't believe it. It was hard to hear over the clamor of the other diners, so I left a twenty on the table and stepped out onto the restaurant's porch.

"If you want me to pursue this, Lacey, I will," he said. "We'll see what we can do to get the surgeries covered."

No doctor had ever made a personal call to me. No doctor had ever said, "I'm going to do what I can to make this happen."

I can't pass that Rafferty's without thinking of Dr. Flores's kindness.

A few months later I received a second personal call from Dr. Flores. Chris leaned in, trying to hear the doctor through the phone.

"Lacey," Dr. Flores said, his voice strong and clear. "I spoke with the medical director of the insurance company personally. If you're ready, let's schedule it. They're covering the surgery."

I called my parents.

I called the hospital to schedule.

I called Marisa.

She was ecstatic and made arrangements for us to stay with her during the surgery. As if she hadn't done enough for us, Marisa made gift bags that included a Team Christian T-shirt and thank-you card for each staff member. When we arrived at the hospital, she distributed them to every member of Dr. Flores's team.

After Christian had been in surgery for a few hours, a staff member gave us an update.

"Everything is going just as planned. Christian is doing fine." She grabbed my hand in such a sweet way. "We're rooting for you and Christian, whatever it takes." Then she lifted up the corner of her professional button-up blouse to show me the royal blue Team Christian shirt peeking out.

That small gesture meant so much to me. The worry I was holding on to melted a little. People were in our corner, people who spend their lives working to help families like ours.

Again I was amazed at God. He was working behind the scenes. I hadn't known how Christian would have these procedures performed, but God did. He'd orchestrated this entire thing, even before Christian was born. He'd allowed these specific people to be working on this day at this time, during the hours that Christian needed the best and the brightest minds, and in the moments when his parents needed a reassuring smile and words of support.

MIRACLE AT 705 RILEY DRIVE

I typically spend the week before Christian's surgeries praying and crying.

Lots of crying.

I ask God to give the doctors the skill and wisdom needed, to have a great night's sleep before the surgery, to guide their hands as they work. I pray for Christian's body to react appropriately to the anesthesia, for God to give him an overwhelming sense of peace, and that pain management won't be a problem. I pray to hold my little boy in my arms after he wakes up.

This second surgery was especially unique. A "hard to close" palate typically ranges from 10mm to 12mm wide. The goal was to close Christian's soft palate, but since it had an 18mm-wide cleft, Dr. Flores didn't think the tissue from each side would reach. The plan was to fill in the gap with tissue from Christian's throat, a pharyngeal flap.

This was a brand-new procedure created specifically for Christian. It had never been done before. We asked for prayer across our social media sites, from our church family, our friends, and loved ones.

I stayed up late and prayed. And cried.

And God showed up.

Before Christian's surgery Dr. Flores met us in one of the side patient rooms. Chris and I sat in the rigid chairs while Christian lay tight against me, clutching my arms.

Chris spoke first. "We think the palate closed a little."

"It honestly looks smaller," I confirmed.

Dr. Flores looked from Chris to me, down at Christian, and then back to Chris. Every millimeter counted. He furrowed his brow momentarily, but ever the professional, he nodded at us. "That just doesn't happen," he said, "but I'll measure to be safe."

Chris carried Christian to the holding, or pre-operating, area. We kissed him and whispered prayers in his ears until a nurse came to get him. I held his hand for as long as I could until he was out of reach. I wanted to chase after them as the nurse carried him in her arms, but I just stood there and cried.

The oceans were rising, and I prayed that God would keep my head above the waves. I trusted Dr. Flores and his incredible surgical team, but I was still terrified of losing my baby.

This surgery was in and of itself the more dangerous of the two—the phalangeal flap of skin from the back of Christian's throat had to be pulled forward. If it swelled, it would block his airway. We had been praying specifically for that part of the procedure to go well.

God answered in bigger ways than we expected.

A few hours later Dr. Flores pushed through the double doors of the surgical area and strode over to us in the waiting room. Everyone moved as close as they could without imposing.

"You'll never believe it," he said, "but the palate *was* narrower than the last surgery. We didn't have to cut the tissue from his throat." The joy on his face was unmistakable as he walked us through the operation. He'd closed the hole just like he would any other cleft palate. He beamed. "Christian was such a champion, such a fighter."

At those words everyone in the waiting area erupted into cheers and applause. As tears fell from my eyes, countless hands grabbed me for hugs. I heard "Praise God, thank You, Father" amidst the noise as our friends and family celebrated and gave God the glory for the successful surgery.

There was no medical explanation for how Christian's palate narrowed, but we believe that God showed mercy upon our son. For that we give Him glory forever. Amen.

The Beauty in Small Gifts

I don't know how to express the joy I felt after Christian's surgeries. Riley Hospital wasn't our first choice, but it was the right choice, and I praise God for His timing. The palate surgeries were critical for Christian. Up until then the hole was so wide that Christian couldn't form words, only mumble. We understood a little of what he was saying, but it was frustrating for him to not be able to communicate.

Two days after the second surgery he called me "Mama" for the first time.

I know it can grow old for a child to repeat "Mommy-Mommy-Mommy," but hearing Christian say Mama never fails to elate my heart. It took so long for those glorious words to ever cross my ears. I relish each syllable. The wait made it even more precious.

I think we honor God when we see beauty in the small gifts He gives us. I took my sight for granted every day of my life until I became the eyes for my child. Hearing other women called "Mommy" in the store never phased me until I drowned in the silence of a child who couldn't say my name.

Dr. Flores changed that for me. He was one of the first people I'd met who truly, 100 percent cared about Christian's outcome. I'll never be able to pay him what he's worth, but I know without a shadow of a doubt that God blesses men and women who care for the least of these.[1]

There are so many people who have shown huge gestures of kindness for Christian. A gentleman by the name of Scot Gilmore wrote a beautiful song for Christian. Titled "No Night," the song is about how Christian's world is always bright because he sees life through the eyes of his heart. We invited him to Christian's second birthday party, where he played it for everyone.

When the song ended, there wasn't a dry eye in the room.

We honor God when we see beauty in the small gifts He gives us.

Scot eventually had the song professionally produced and put on iTunes. He donates the proceeds to Christian.[*]

Another precious friend is Mr. Joshua York. We met through Facebook, and when he knew we would be in his hometown of Indianapolis, he invited us to come hear him play the piano. We showed up at a McDonald's that has a large grand piano set up right in the restaurant and watched the sweet blind man tickle the ivories with passion and vigor.

For both of Christian's Indy surgeries, Mr. Joshua came and sat with us in the waiting room. He lets us ask questions about vision impairments and gives us perspective on what it was like to grow up blind.

Mr. Joshua also gives the best advice on how to raise Christian!

---

* If you want to download "No Night," visit http://charitysongs.org/lacy--christian -buchanan.html.

He uses a cane for mobility, and I have watched him use his iPhone in the accessibility mode. I think it's neat to watch how Christian will one day be able to use technology!

EVERY KINDNESS MATTERS

I would be remiss to not include a few of the extra kindnesses we received from staff members at Riley Hospital for Children. Because we'd had some terrible experiences at our other hospital, each gesture made an incredible impact on my heart. I learned that there are no insignificant acts of thoughtfulness.

When we were at the hospital to clear up an ear infection before an upcoming surgery, a nurse handed Christian her iPhone so he could listen to Disney music. I was amazed that she trusted him with an expensive device.

Before Christian's first palate surgery the staff wheeled a mini grand piano into the waiting area. Christian flipped his Superman cape when he sat, just like a master pianist flares his tuxedo tails behind the piano bench.

The chatter in the waiting area stilled as my son began to play. When he finished, everyone clapped. It was a beautiful moment, all because someone took the initiative to calm a little boy before surgery.

Another example is when a staff member brought an ExerSaucer activity center for Chandler to sit in while Christian had an operation. It was a huge blessing for Chandler to be occupied. He bounced and laughed, and I knew he was safe and contained, which made the waiting a little easier.

There are seriously hundreds of stories to share. Although Christian is too young to understand their impact, I hope to raise him in such a way that not only honors God but also represents my immense gratitude for these precious gifts from strangers.

Chapter Thirteen

MEDIA FRENZY

Everywhere you look you see people searching for love ... but they're looking in the wrong places. God is love, and they will never find what they're looking for until they find Him.
—JOYCE MEYER

W E WEREN'T PREPARED for the media storm that rained over us after the video went viral. It seemed to be a ripple effect. One newspaper would write an article, then a different paper wrote their spin, and so on and so on. I received numerous e-mails and phone calls from people requesting interviews. Writers in the United Kingdom got in touch with me, and we did several newspaper and magazine interviews.

One day I received a call from Jessica Bliss, a reporter from our local paper, *The Tennessean*. She'd seen our feature in the

Murfreesboro, Tennessee, *Daily News Journal* and wanted to know if she could shadow us for a day.

When Chris and I decided to love and educate people who asked questions about Christian's disability, we had no idea God would expand our reach further than the curious stranger at the grocery store. I looked at each interview opportunity as a gift from God, so I agreed.

We set up a date, and I called ahead to our appointments for that day to get permission for photos to be taken. The privacy of the other families was a concern of mine, so we nailed down some terms and were given the green light.

Our first stop was Christian's pediatrician for his annual well visit. We chatted in the waiting area while Christian occupied himself with some toys. In the article that Jessica wrote, she captured a snapshot in time of how other children reacted to Christian.

She described how the other kids moved away from the toy table when Christian walked over to the play area. He ran his fingers over the smooth plastic, then bowed his head when he realized he was standing there alone.

I hadn't thought much of this moment; I'd seen it before. I was used to children being wary of my son. They weren't trying to be cruel. They've never seen a kid who looks like Christian, so what do I expect them to do? I wait to see if kids will work it out themselves, or if I need to intervene. But this was Jessica's first experience, and she left her seat to join him. She squatted beside Christian and guided his hand along one of the toys.

I saw a meme on Facebook that said, "Fill your child's confidence bucket so full that when people poke holes in it, it doesn't empty." Christian began dealing with rejection at such a young age that I use these moments to build him up so that when his feelings get hurt, it takes a lot to knock him down.

This is a delicate balance, so we praise and comfort when

necessary. Chris and I want Christian to know that his worth comes from who God made him, not what he looks like, and he is amazing, special, wonderful, and awesome. He's still so young, so I'm trying to lay that foundation so that when bigger issues arise, we can build on it.

THE DOCTORS

Our biggest media appearance to date was on the hit television show *The Doctors*. When they called and asked to film Christian's first surgery at Riley Hospital for a documentary, I was thrilled. They gave me an opportunity to see what happens behind the closed doors of the operating room.

Their team was incredible. We sat for interviews before the surgery so they could get the backstory on Christian and all the medical details. Then they came with us to Riley and filmed. During the surgery the crew was extremely supportive. I was a nervous wreck, of course, but they were kind and compassionate.

I thought it was the end of our time with them, but that next January I received a second call. They wanted to know if we could fly out that week to appear on the show.

"When do you want us?" I said.

"Thursday."

It was Monday.

"Let me make some calls!" I got off the phone and called Chris immediately. Chandler was still nursing, so I couldn't go alone. Thankfully Chris's boss gave him the time off, again showing flexibility when it came to Christian's schedule.

Lacey Buchanan
January 9, 2014

OK, prayer warrior friends. It's time to spill the beans. Our family has been offered an amazing opportunity to go to Hollywood, California, to be on The Doctors. Of course we said yes. Please be in prayer for us as we travel and share Christian with more people. Any of you who know me know my fear of flying is extreme. Please pray for safe travels, peace, and God's will.

I rearranged Christian's appointments for the week, threw our clothes and supplies into suitcases, and we hopped on a plane to California. After two layovers we arrived in sunny Los Angeles wearing our winter clothes. After we underwent a quick costume change, the crew took us to In-and-Out Burger for dinner (a new tradition for us when we visit California), to the studio for filming, then dropped us off at the hotel.

SIGHTSEEING

We'd packed in such a rush that I forgot the most important toiletry product for contact lens wearers. Saline solution.

We had the whole next day free to explore the city, so we ran to the closest drugstore and I grabbed a bottle. That next morning I popped one of my contacts into my eye and screamed. It felt like I'd splashed my eye with acid.

Holding my palm against my eye while tears streamed down my cheeks, I grabbed the bottle of lens solution. Only it wasn't saline. I'd grabbed a bottle of contact cleanser by mistake.

I flushed my eye with water for about five minutes, then lay on the bed with a compress. After about an hour my eye was still swollen and red—and we were filming *The Doctors* episode the next day. I was mortified that I would be on TV with one bright red eyeball.

Chris and the boys patiently waited for my eye to clear a bit. Determined not to let this ruin our day, I grabbed my glasses, and off we went to sightsee.

We had the best time as we snapped a ton of pictures on the Hollywood Walk of Fame, stepped in our favorite celebrities' cement-cast footprints, and enjoyed every tourist-y moment, including the open-van tour. The boys couldn't have cared less as we rode all over Hollywood, although Christian loved the breeze against his face.

We passed George Clooney's aunt's house (coolest thing ever) and drove down Sunset Boulevard with all the fabulous clothing shops that only the stars can afford. That evening one of the ladies from Riley's public relations office took us to dinner, then we collapsed into bed.

On Set

The next morning we drove into Paramount Studios and marveled over the famous water tower. #Tourists

As soon as we arrived on the set, a special nanny took Christian and Chandler to our dressing room to play while crew members escorted Chris and me to the hair and makeup department. This was not an opportunity I was going to waste. As the makeup artist worked, I asked him for tips, and I'll share one now: eyebrow makeup needs to be one shade darker than the natural eyebrow color.

"I didn't even know there was such a thing as eyebrow makeup," said the country girl in the big city. He laughed, and after a few minutes he let me see myself in the mirror.

My eyes looked bigger somehow, and my skin was practically

airbrushed. It was incredible. He wished me good luck and passed me on to the hair team.

I didn't know that anyone was going to do my hair, so that morning I'd woken up early to straighten it. I sat in the swivel chair, and the stylists gave me a thorough once-over.

"It looks so pretty," one of them said. "I don't think we need to do anything."

"Did a professional just say I did my hair well?" I joked.

Best. Compliment. Ever.

They curled loose waves to frame my face, then handed me over to the wardrobe department. They'd asked our sizes, so I went into the small dressing room to change into an emerald top and black slacks. Chris joined me a moment later, dashing in a charcoal suit that accentuated his broad shoulders.

The boys had a play area in one part of the dressing room, so we left Chandler playing happily in the care of the nanny. Together Chris, Christian, and I waited in the backstage area for our cue.

When they announced us, we walked onto the set in front of a live audience. It was smaller than I'd expected. The television made it appear so large. Chris and I were nervous, but Christian was fearless. He wanted to explore, so while I answered Dr. Travis Stork's questions, the other doctors kept Christian entertained as he walked around and around the coffee table and across the stage.

The audience loved him. They laughed and *awww'd*. He could have burped, and they would have thought it was the greatest thing ever. At one point Christian walked toward the sound of their voices and almost fell off the stage. Several members of the audience rushed to catch him, but we grabbed him just in time.

After a few questions Dr. Travis introduced Dr. Flores, who'd flown in as a special guest for the taping. We were thrilled to see him, and he answered their questions with grace and charm. Par for the course, as always.

God Goes Big

Before the segment ended, we received one of the greatest surprises of our lives. *The Doctors* partnered with the Dr. Phil Foundation to accept donations to offset the costs of Christian's surgeries. The money they raised went into a special needs trust for Christian. The joy of knowing my baby could receive the best care possible and knowing we had the top-notch surgeon in our corner felt so unreal. It was more than an answer to prayer because I hadn't prayed that big. I'd asked God to heal Christian, yes, but when I prayed over our finances, I was always looking just a little bit ahead.

When our God goes big, He goes all the way.

The taping ended, and we got pictures with the stars backstage. On set I'd sat next to Dr. Travis, who is totally dreamy, by the way, and super nice. I have one picture of me sitting next to him during the interview where it looks like I'm staring at him like a schoolgirl. One of my friends made a meme out of it. She zoomed in three times and captioned it: *The face you make when you can smell Dr. Travis.* The funniest part is that Chris squinted at the exact second the picture was taken so it looks like I have a jealous husband behind me.

Piano Lessons

On the episode of *The Doctors* we shared with the world how talented Christian is on the piano. It felt awesome to brag on my little boy, to declare how bright he is. After all, my blind child could play the beginning bars of "Für Elise."

After only four lessons.

At the age of two.

He's been able to pick out melodies for years.

For instance, one day I was washing dishes and his nurse was filling out paperwork, when Christian jumped up from where he was playing on the floor and took off toward the piano. He doesn't normally move fast, so his nurse and I stopped in the middle of what we were doing to watch. Christian sat on the bench then picked out the tune: Bum bum bum. Bum bum bum. Ba da bum—bum bum.

"Jingle Bells."

I'd never heard him play it before. Ever.

His nurse and I looked at each other, jaws dropped, then we cheered. I convinced him to do it again so I could film it. To share that on national television was such a proud parent moment.

WishTV.com picked up our story after we were on *The Doctors*. I was a bit more emotional during this taping because their interview was actually filmed while Christian was in surgery. When I'd explained the timing of their request, they were really sweet and said we could do it another time, but it was nice to have something to think about besides the fact that my child was under anesthesia.

They did a great job building up Riley Hospital, which I was thankful for. The community in Indianapolis is proud of Riley, and it was great to give them the kudos and publicity they deserve.

SPEAKING ENGAGEMENTS

Raising awareness for the disabled community became my calling. I stopped taking speaking engagements for this past year because I was getting ready for the bar exam, but before that we traveled at least once a month.

We saw this as part of our adventure. I was blessed to speak in Lynchburg, Virginia, where Liberty University is located, as well as in Chillicothe, Ohio, for a Goodwill event honoring their employees, many of whom are disabled. They were really great to us.

We've been to San Francisco and Los Angeles (for *The Doctors*). I spoke at a banquet about a five-hour drive away in northeastern Kentucky, where it snowed six to eight inches, which is so rare for our part of the country. Normally we'll have an inch or two at the most. The boys experienced the snow in small doses. Christian gets cold easily and doesn't like to be chilled. But he'd play in the snow forever if it wasn't cold!

BAD PUBLICITY

Not all of our media frenzy experience has been positive. So many comments on YouTube were heinous and hateful. We've been accused of pimping Christian's story so we could become famous, that I'm using Christian for celebrity status.

I care, to a point, about what people think, and I try to be extremely careful about what I say online, which means I avoid some topics altogether. For example, there is a certain group of people who think if plastic surgery can make a child look more normal, it should be done. My blog post titled "Why My Child Won't Get Cosmetic Surgery" received a lot of negative backlash when I said I don't want to make Christian undergo all these surgeries to give him prosthetic eyes just to make other people comfortable with the way he looks.

My theory is that I'm not concerned about my kids being like everyone else. I feel like people get so caught up with fitting in that they don't stop to think that maybe they're not supposed to. Fitting in is so overrated. It's not on my priority list, and it's not on my kids'.

The world is in shambles, following whatever the TV says, buying whatever commercials say to buy. It reminds me of the movie *Wall-E*. I'm trying to raise world-changers who follow Jesus, not society.

From Weeping to Joy

To say life changed for the Buchanan family after the media frenzy is an understatement. When we walked out of Paramount Studios after *The Doctors* filming, a man came over to me and said, "My wife follows you on Facebook! Can I get my picture with you? She is going to flip out!"

Before the viral video people approached us in public because they wanted to know, "What's wrong with your baby?" After the video they approached because they *recognized* him. "Oh my gosh—that's Christian!" I liked this reaction a million times more.

> People get so caught up with fitting in that they don't stop to think that maybe they're not supposed to.

God turned my weeping into joy. It used to be so hard to go out and deal with people, but now it's fun. Instead of whispers and stares, people apologize for wanting to talk to us.

"I don't want to bother you."

I look them square in the eye with a smile and say, "No, you are *not* bothering us. We love it."

I'll never take for granted the politeness of the people in our town. They've embraced Christian and will stop me in the store to remind me how and when they met him for the first time. Instead of being worried that he'll be teased, which I know will happen, I'm now more at ease in public knowing that he'll also hear the awed voices of people who admire and love him.

Strangers weren't the only ones embracing our family, of course. Our friends constantly lifted us up with prayer and support.

One time a friend and I got separated in Old Navy. I headed toward the front entrance at the same time she walked around a corner and we bumped into each other.

"Oh my gosh. It's Lacey Buchanan!" she teased.

I gave her arm a little smack and headed to the checkout.

Other friends will give us a hard time if someone approaches us while we're together. Their joking is all in good fun because they were there during the bitter times. They are so thankful that we're raising awareness and receive a different reaction when we're out and about.

They love Christian, and for him to become a mini-celebrity in our hometown is nothing short of God making good on His unspoken command not to hide this baby.

A REDEMPTION STORY

I'll never forget the day that college boy drove me to tears after insisting on seeing Christian. The wound stayed open and fresh for a long time. Every time I remembered his horrified gasp, my heart hurt.

God turned my weeping into joy.

The God we serve heals.

The Great Physician repairs.

When Christian was three years old, our family went back to that same small Walmart on our way home from an appointment. I tensed a little as we went inside but brushed the memory to the back of my mind.

As we walked out to the parking lot after shopping, a woman and a little girl approached.

"We follow you on Facebook, and my daughter wanted to meet you," the woman said. "Do you mind if we take a picture?"

God rescued a painful memory that I'd buried in the recesses of my heart, dusted it off, and attached a new ending.

He is the Redeemer of hearts.

The Redeemer of souls.

The Redeemer of moments.

Chapter Fourteen

ANOTHER BUCHANAN BABY!

How mighty, how great the One must be, I thought,
to send the heavens careening, and yet hear the cry
of a single heart.
—TOSCA LEE, *HAVAH: THE STORY OF EVE*

THE NEWS OF baby number two came as a perfectly timed surprise during our Ohio travels. On our way to Shriners Hospital in Cincinnati waves of nausea passed over me, and I knew something was off. Give me the craziest roller coaster, and I'll tame it like a wild pony. However, we were driving straight down the highway, no twists or curves, but I thought I was going to vomit all over Julie's car.

And I knew.

I turned my cell phone to silent, then discreetly texted Chris. Two feet away. In the backseat.

I'm pregnant.

He texted back: *How do you know?*

I just know.

Did you miss your period?

No, but I know.

I turned my phone upside down on my leg in case he texted back and willed myself to keep my breakfast down. I couldn't repay Julie's kindness by vomiting in her car.

The day was full of appointments, so Chris and I didn't get a chance to talk privately until after dinner at Julie's house. Chris leaned over and whispered, "I'm going to go get a test."

This was completely embarrassing. "You can't go get a pregnancy test!" I hissed. It felt like we were teenagers hiding from my mother. What would Julie think of us if she found a pregnancy test in her trash can?

"I have to know," he said.

Chris grabbed his coat. "I'm headed to Starbucks. Gonna get Lacey a coffee."

Under the guise of my caffeine cravings he bought a test from the store, grabbed a Mocha Frappuccino to avoid suspicion, then impatiently waited for me to fill my bladder so I could take the test.

Negative.

He continued this James Bond routine for three days straight. Each time the test came back negative, but despite the solitary pink line on the stick, I knew I was pregnant.

On the fourth day I was so frustrated that I bought a test at a gas station after an appointment and took it then and there. Still negative.

On the last day of our visit Chris pulled the Starbucks charade a final time. The fifth time's a charm, I guess, because finally two dark pink lines showed up.

Sharing the News

This second pregnancy was beautifully typical—morning sickness, food cravings, mood swings. I'm sure I was fatigued, but with law school and Christian's appointments, I was already exhausted. I tried to rest when Christian did, but that usually meant I reclined on the bed while I studied instead of actually napping.

I was already nervous about being able to handle two little ones. And what if this baby had special needs too? Was I strong enough to handle it? Would God give me the strength I required? I knew He would, but the fears niggled the back of my brain.

Christian was eighteen months old when I got pregnant, but he was only between eight and ten months old developmentally. When we told him I had a baby in my tummy, he didn't fully understand. Several times throughout the day, I would say, "Mama is having a baby!" and place his hand on my stomach.

When I started showing more, Chris or I would say, "Christian, rub the baby," and he did. Then he would smack it.

Whenever we said, "Don't smack the baby!," he'd throw his head back and laugh. Just like siblings, I guess. He'd pretend to love the baby, then pop!

When my sister-in-law invited us over to their house for dinner, I knew we had the perfect opportunity to do a family reveal. My brother, Dustin, lives in the house smack-dab next door to my parents, so in keeping with the Superman theme, I bought Christian a shirt off of Etsy (*I love Etsy!*) that said, "I'm going to be a Super Big Brother."

No one noticed his shirt when we walked in, so Chris and I gave each other a look and waited. I was dying for someone to notice, but supper was served and still nothing. Chris and I shot nervous glances at each other across the table: *How are they not seeing this? Should we say something?*

I knew Chris wouldn't be able to contain the secret much longer. Thankfully, in the middle of dinner, my sister-in-law, Jessica, blurted out, "Are you pregnant?"

Immediately conversations ended. Everyone's heads snapped to look at me.

"Why did you say that?" I said.

"Christian's shirt."

Everyone simultaneously turned and looked at him. My mom threw her hands in the air and ran over to hug me. The congratulations flowed, and hugs, tears, and happiness filled the rest of the evening.

ANOTHER ROUND OF ULTRASOUNDS

Because of Christian's birth defect, I was considered a high-risk pregnancy, which meant one happy thing. More ultrasounds.

I never tired of watching my children in utero. The level of detail we saw, this tiny window of intrusion as God knit our babies together, always amazed me.

Finally the day of the anatomy ultrasound appointment arrived. I couldn't wait to find out if we were having a boy or girl. But even more importantly, we would know if this baby had any indications of a cleft palate. The words "I don't care what we're having as long as it's healthy" were never truer. (Although I was convinced I was having a girl.)

When I went for the scan, the same perinatologist who monitored Christian's scans came into the exam room. We spent the first few minutes catching him up on Christian's progress. It was amazing to be back with this doctor for the second addition to our family. We love him so much we almost used his first name for Chandler's middle name!

He specifically checked the baby's orbital areas. The amniotic bands had pinned Christian's face to the placenta, so this was the moment of truth. Even after all of Christian's ultrasounds, I still couldn't decipher the details the tech and doctor could see.

After a few minutes the doctor pointed out a darker shadow on the screen.

"That's the lens," he said. "Everything looks perfect."

The tech turned up the volume dial, and we listened to a perfect heartbeat as we thanked God for perfect eyelids. After a few minutes she turned down the sound and asked the big question.

"Do you want to know the gender, or do you want to wait?"

We wanted to wait. The next day we were meeting with our photographer friend Gina to take gender reveal photos. I wanted to capture the moment when I found out if my baby was a boy or a girl.

"You guys turn your heads for a couple of minutes while I get some measurements," she said. "I'll take some pictures and then write the gender down and seal it in an envelope."

Chris and I turned our heads. After a couple of minutes she gave us the OK to look at the screen again. When the tech finished, she vacated the room momentarily to seal the results.

We left the appointment with a precious envelope in my purse. Chris pretended to sneak a peek once we got into the car, and I threatened to throw it out the window if he tried again, so neither of us would know.

Truce.

We drove to Gina's house, slipped her the envelope, and went home. I was secretly jealous that she knew before I did, but I was super excited about the photo shoot. Tomorrow couldn't come fast enough.

THE GENDER REVEAL

I wish we'd known about gender reveal parties when I was pregnant with Christian, but it really wasn't a thing even just a couple of years before. Gina's spectacular theme idea was: "Every superhero has a sidekick."

The next day we met at the park so we'd have a pretty background for the pictures. Since it was November, Gina had filled a giant box wrapped in Christmas paper with balloons.

It was a gorgeous day. I couldn't have asked for more perfect weather. There was a slight chill in the air, and the breeze gave my hair that windblown tousle I could never achieve at home.

Chris and I stood behind the box and waited for her to get into position. I placed my hands on the lid, and he did the same. Gina counted to three, and Chris and I opened the lid together.

I was totally shocked when powder blue helium balloons burst forth, but I wasn't the least bit disappointed. I watched them fly to the tops of the trees and beyond.

Magical.

Gina gave us the full treatment, posing us in different positions. She was amazing with Christian and so patient when he wanted to do anything but sit still. I treasure these photos intensely. Christian was going to have a brother, and I was going to be even more outnumbered.

CHOOSING A NAME

Names are incredibly impactful, and I wanted my baby's name to carry deep meaning. Christian's name means "follower of Christ," which I love.

I'd been so sure that I was having a girl that I didn't have a boy name picked out. In fact, I was already calling my baby by the girl name!

One evening my mom called me out of the blue.

"I know your baby's name."

I wasn't sure if grandparents got to pick the names of both their own babies *and* the grandchildren, but I played along.

"OK, tell me."

"Chandler."

Yes.

As soon as I got off the phone, I googled the meaning of the name Chandler.

Candle-maker.

That wasn't what I was expecting. Yet my baby's name was Chandler, candle-maker or not.

And Chandler needed a room, so we got busy and worked on the nursery. Chris and I wanted the boys to be near each other and also for us to have some privacy, so we converted the master bedroom into Chandler's room and moved our stuff into the much larger den on the other side of the house.

In keeping with Christian's color scheme of mostly blue with hints of brown, we reversed the colors for Chandler. Chris is super handy, so we painted the bottom half of the wall a beautiful mocha, the top half a smooth *caffè crema*, and installed a white chair railing along the seam where the two colors met. We went to Hobby Lobby (like I needed an excuse) and purchased the wooden letters to spell out his name above the crib just as we did in Christian's room.

I loved how coordinated the boys' rooms were becoming, but the *aha* moment was when I found the same exact blue curtains that were on Christian's windows—in brown. As a finishing piece we rolled out a geometric patterned rug in tans and browns to tie everything together.

A couple of months later I was at a friend's house for her birthday party. I was far along into the pregnancy by then, so my friends would touch my belly hoping for a kick from Chandler. We were chatting easily in the kitchen when the birthday girl randomly asked me if I'd chosen a name. Her eyes lit up when I told her.

She set her glass of punch on the island. "That's a family name of ours. Do you know the meaning?"

"Candle-maker. It's derived from *chandelier*," I said.

She shook her head. "No, it means 'the one who brings the light.'"

RENEWED JOY

Chandler's pregnancy brought a renewed joy to our lives and a tether Chris and I used to pull each other closer. In the midst of endless appointments, procedures, and paperwork, the days carried the thrill of new life. A fresh starting point. Babies have a way of making the world seem brighter.

> She thanked God that life was not always winter, that spring always came at last to chase away the cold and heaviness, and to release one to warmth and movement again.[1]

Even chores felt like rewards. We unpacked Christian's old baby clothes and delighted in how tiny they were. How could he have ever been that small? I washed, folded, and carefully put away the hand-me-downs, set up the diaper-changing station, and arranged all the little bottles of lotions and creams.

As I worked, I'd have flashes of doing these same motions, the same system for Christian, and my heart felt as if it would grow too large for my body to contain. I'd thought I could never love anyone the way I loved Christian, but here was another Buchanan baby who already was loved to pieces. I don't know how to explain it—I'm not sure anyone does—but God absolutely allows an abundance of love for every child. I look at both of my boys and wonder how I ever got chosen to be the mother of these two precious souls.

A baby brings a comfort to the family.

This baby brought a marriage together.

There's a verse in the Old Testament that I cling to, Joel 2:25: "I will repay you for the years the locusts have eaten—the great locust and the young locust, the other locusts and the locust swarm—my great army that I sent among you" (NIV).

It doesn't carry the same impact today as it did back in those ancient times, since the majority of us don't lose our livelihood to locust infestation. But we do miss out on special events, moments that are taken for granted until they are stolen.

In a lot of ways blessing us with Chandler was God's way of restoring the typical mommy experience that I missed out on with Christian. I felt impressed upon my heart that God said, "I'm repaying you for the years the locusts have eaten."

I'd lost once-in-a-lifetime moments with my firstborn, but our God is a gracious and loving Father who saw fit to give me the desires of my heart. I wanted to experience a natural birth instead of another C-section. I wanted to claim the first precious moments of Chandler's life with him in my arms instead of having him taken from me for hours. I wanted newborn pictures instead of blank, empty pages in the baby book. I wanted my family and best friends to celebrate immediately with us, together, instead of escorting them one by one to a small, sad room.

Instead of praying specifically for those things, I asked God instead to keep Chandler healthy and whole. At that time I didn't feel like I had a right to ask for anything else, but our God is generous and loving.

These small, unspoken yearnings made it to God's ears, and He worked out each one of those requests so that my heart would be satisfied and I would praise the name of my God who dealt wondrously with me.[2]

MUSTACHE TAKEOVER

My friends went mustache crazy.

They threw Chandler a baby shower with an "I'm a Little Man" theme, and with the popularity of mustache décor it was perfect timing. The straws had paper mustaches attached so it looked like you had a mustache while you sipped through one. Mustache décor covered the church, and when guests arrived, they were handed mustache stickers to adhere to their outfits.

My aunt Joan was again in charge of the dessert. She is an amazing cook and created a gorgeous truffle cake with a blue mousse and alternating layers of crushed Oreos. That sat next to the blue frosted cupcakes with mustache toothpicks.

In one corner of the room my friends set up a photo booth station with a chalkboard to write notes and various silly accessories and props. And, of course, mustaches. My 103-year-old grandma got into the action and held up mustache disguises in the photo booth. She was a spritely woman. When she was in her eighties she would chase Dustin and me around the front yard during games of hide-and-seek. Chandler's baby shower is one of the last few precious memories I have with her before God called her to heaven three months after Chandler was born.

In keeping with my no-cheesy-game wishes, my friends devised an activity consisting of a single diaper and a Sharpie. The rule was simple: write on the diaper a middle-of-the-night pep talk. They collected the diapers in a beautiful special basket so I couldn't read them ahead of time.

After Chandler was born, I actually looked forward to those late-night changes. I'd dim the light in Chandler's room, pull out one of the special diapers, and laugh over the crazy sayings. One of my aunts wrote, "Call Aunt Karen to come change this diaper." One of my friends penned, "I hope this poop isn't too big." Those pep talks were some of my favorite things.

WELCOME, BABY CHANDLER

My little boy arrived eight days past his due date, which is par for the course for Chandler. To have a VBAC (vaginal birth after cesarean), my body had to go into labor on its own. The doctors gave me a ten-day window before I'd have to have a C-section. Sure enough, we scheduled the C-section for May 16, and he came two days before that date.

Cutting it close there, kid!

My contractions came in less than ten minute increments for three days, starting at nine o'clock on Saturday evening and ending on Tuesday at 8:16 p.m. when he took his first breath. On Tuesday morning my aunt drove me to the hospital and Chris went to work as normal, just in case I wasn't dilated, with strict instructions to call him the moment I knew anything.

We got settled into an exam room and waited for the nurse to check my progress. She smiled, "You're gonna have a baby today!"

I called Chris, but he didn't answer his cell or work phone. My only other option was to call his department and get a random person on the line. A sweet-sounding girl answered.

"Hi, my husband works in your department. Chris Buchanan. I'm in labor and he's not answering the phone. I know it's not part of your job, but could you find him please?"

She congratulated me, then got off the line, promising to find him.

A few minutes later Chris called my phone, immediately apologizing for not hearing it while he was getting breakfast. Of all things.

Chandler was born later that evening, and just as I'd hoped, the doctor immediately laid him on my chest. I nursed him, changed his diapers, and slipped the tiniest of socks on his feet after marveling over the slender adorable toes.

I got to be his mom.

Christian came to visit, wearing his favorite Elmo jammies. I held Chandler in the crook of my arm while Christian placed his hands on his newborn brother. "This is Chandler; this is your brother," we told him, stroking his fingers against Chandler's cheek.

My boys. My family.

The brotherly love didn't last long. A couple of days later we brought Chandler home and let Christian hold him. We gently set Chandler in Christian's lap and stayed right beside the boys.

"Christian, love the baby. That's your brother! Give him love!"

Without missing a beat, Christian pushed Chandler out of his lap.

Thankfully Chris and I had prepared, so Chandler scooted right into Daddy's open hands.

Their first official get-together captured their relationship perfectly. Three years later they're still wrestling.

 Lacey Buchanan
May 20, 2013

Chandler and I are awake nursing and he passes gas so loud it wakes Chris up beside us! Hahahahahaha!!!! He gets that trait from his dad.

TYPICAL TODDLERS

Raising Chandler gave us a lot of insight into what it's like to have a child hit the age milestones at the right time. Christian was

twenty-seven months old when Chandler was born, but developmentally he was only around ten to twelve months old. He wasn't
talking or walking yet, so sometimes it felt like we had two children the same age.

Chandler is the definition of *boy* in every sense of the word.
At times he pushes my buttons, but I wouldn't change a thing.
Typical toddler experiences are what I longed for. As a small
example, I wanted to make mud pies with my kids, but Christian
has sensory issues and won't touch Play-Doh, dirt, or paint. God
used Chandler to fill those empty spaces.

The child knows no fear. If Christian was walking toward a
busy road, Chandler would be like, "Oh cool, I'll go with you."
If I tell him not to touch something, he'll watch me and slowly
move toward the forbidden object. When he's told to stop, he
laughs a deep belly giggle and does it again. Instead of playing at
the kiddie table, Chandler conquers, standing on top of it until
someone pulls him off.

Chandler learned to pull himself upright at eight months old.
Christian's development took longer, so I had not grown accustomed to the Houdini-like behaviors of a small curious infant.
After dinner one day I threw some fried chicken into the trash,
wiped the counter, and left the kitchen. I came right back, but in
the few moments I was gone, Chandler had grabbed the chicken
out of the trash can and was sitting on the floor in his footed
jammies munching on a chicken wing.

He also filled holes in his brother's life. Chandler taught
Christian how to be a little boy. He showed Christian how to
climb onto the counter and turn on the water faucet. Christian
repaid him by opening the front door while I was in the bathroom and letting him outdoors. Two-year-old Chandler was
happy to oblige. Thankfully our neighbor saw Chandler on the

porch, picked him up, and filled me in when I walked back into the living room.

Recently when I told the boys to smile for a picture, Chandler grabbed Christian's hand, then closed his eyes and stood there. I don't know if he was pretending to be blind or what. Instead of holding things out to Christian, Chandler knows to say "here" and put items directly in Christian's hands. He's never indicated that Christian looks different from anyone else.

There's a lesson to be learned in how Chandler treats Christian. He's not any different—he's just Christian. And that's OK.

Lacey Buchanan
June 12, 2015

Chandler purposefully snuggled up to Christian tonight to fall to sleep. Sometimes I worry about their bond because Christian doesn't understand how to interact with Chandler and Chandler can't figure out why Christian won't talk to him or make eye contact. I worry about all those little things with the boys and then this happens. My heart is full of love.

I'm truly blessed that both boys are mama's boys. They love to wrestle with Daddy and are so excited to see him when he comes home. But if they are sick or need something, they want Mama for sure.

I feel like Chandler was God's way of helping me trust Him. When Christian was little, I couldn't enjoy the day-to-day. I've always felt I had to be on high alert and protect him from everyone and everything because I couldn't trust anyone to do the right thing. With all the mistreatments, misdiagnoses, and hateful comments, I became Marlin in *Finding Nemo*. Hyper-vigilant and overprotective.

For the past few years everything felt so out of control: my marriage, Christian's health, doctors. Life wasn't supposed to be this way. When I felt like I was in a tailspin, I tried to control meaningless things by decreeing, "Nobody is allowed to watch my kid except these two people," or, "We won't see that specialist." I had to find the "perfect" doctor.

Honestly I never had control. It was a false illusion. God knows what we need, which is why He gave us Chandler.

Chandler, who is mischief incarnate.

Chandler, who is noise covered in dirt.[3]

Chandler, who taught me to laugh again.

Chapter Fifteen

GROWING UP

*God is in control, and therefore in everything I can give
thanks—not because of the situation but because of the
One who directs and rules over it.*
—KAY ARTHUR, *As Silver Refined*

H APPY BIRTHDAY TO Christian!"
The waitress set a beautiful thick slice of vanilla cake
on the table in front of him. A candle glowed from
its place of honor in the center of the creamy ganache frosting.
Crimson syrup swirls adorned the plate, and two perky mint
sprigs cocooned a tiny helping of fresh raspberries.

Chris and I clapped, Chandler laughed, and Christian grinned.
I bent down close so he could hear me above the chatter and din
of the other diners.

"They gave you a birthday cake. There is a candle with fire on
top. You get to blow it out and make a wish."

He reached out, and I carefully put his fingers on the edge of the plate.

"Can you blow, Christian?" This is a skill we were still working on. He stuck out his lips in an imitation of what he'd felt ours do when we tried to teach him. I winked at Chris, then softly blew out the candle.

Christian sniffed as the flame extinguished, a trail of white and gray smoke in its place.

"Yay!" we cheered. I gave him a squeeze, kissed his cheek, and thanked God for the last five precious years of my boy's life.

Christian has come a long way since that first surgery in the NICU. His short life has been a constant roller coaster, yet he has the sweetest disposition. So far his experiences have made him a tough little guy with no indication that he harbors any anger for what he's had to go through.

Chris and I want our boys to grow up to be productive, contributing members of society. While we give them grace and freedom to be rough-and-tumble little boys, we don't overly baby them. Christian is extremely intelligent, despite being a little developmentally behind kids his age. Our fear was that if Christian went to a public school, he'd be given a pass to coast by because he was the blind kid. I don't want people to underestimate or coddle him.

We had a couple of options for Christian's education. One was the Tennessee School for the Blind (TSB) in Nashville (an hour-and-a-half drive from Woodbury) or a local school that had great reviews but not a program specifically for sight-impaired children. It seemed like an easy decision. Obviously the school for blind children is in Christian's best interest, but weighed against the savings of gas money and time, and Chandler eventually being in a different school, the local option was pretty tempting. For a hot minute.

While it would be lovely to not drive so far every day, distance isn't a determining factor compared to the specialized care Christian receives in Nashville. I won't cheat him of this educational opportunity because I don't want to be in the car.

It was clear we'd made the right choice. We knew Christian would receive an evaluation at the Tennessee School for the Blind, and I was excited to learn the results. Comparing Christian to kids his own age who can see wouldn't provide an accurate assessment. So in 2015 they ranked him against other blind kids his age to determine where he was developmentally.

His evaluation week was incredible. We loved their state-of-the-art playground, and Christian's assessment results gave us a clear plan to follow.

 Lacey Buchanan
June 11, 2015

Day 4 of Tennessee School for the Blind Summer Evaluation Program is under way!!!! Woo-hoo! Christian has done AMAZING and really impressed his teachers!

We saw firsthand that the instructors treated their charges like any other child. They know what these kids are capable of and are trained and ready to handle any situation.

This was the school for us.

SUMMER CAMP

In the summer of 2016 Christian attended Bell Academy's annual summer camp at Middle Tennessee State University (MTSU), my alma mater, courtesy of the National Federation for the Blind (NFB), Tennessee Chapter. Each morning we woke up around six o'clock, ate breakfast, got dressed, and climbed into the car for the ride to camp. Thankfully the drive was only half an hour.

Sometimes I think it would be wonderful to move closer to all of Christian's therapies and his school. But then on the ride back we enter Woodbury, and it feels like home.

Christian's teacher let us know that the kids would be learning how to use what is called a white cane. The NFB provides complimentary canes that can be replaced every six months to children who are blind. Christian has only had one, since when I try to get him to use it, he drops it wherever he's standing and walks away.

I warned his teacher when we arrived for the first day that we'd had a lot of difficulty providing the right motivation for him. She nodded understandingly. I wasn't the first parent to deal with little ones who ignored their parents. It felt strangely nice to be part of that group, even though it meant our kids were stinkers.

When I picked Christian up after camp, I watched him playing with toys. I knew if he heard my voice that he'd be happy to see me, but going home meant tears if he didn't want to leave.

I called his name, and he came over to me with the biggest grin. I scooped him into my arms and hugged him tightly. The full day of camp was the longest we'd been apart, except for surgeries and NICU overnights—and in those instances he'd been asleep. I'd missed part of his experiences, and I wanted to know every moment of his day.

His teacher reminded Christian to get his cane from his cubby, then leaned into me.

"We had no problems with his cane," she said. "He listened to all the directions with no fussing."

Of course he did.

As much as people assume otherwise, Christian is as typical as any other kid who is more willing to listen to anyone besides a parent. He has zero qualms telling me no if he doesn't want to do something. I've had to sit him in time-out for screaming at me, but he wouldn't dream of yelling at his teachers. As I waited at the camp for Christian to come back from his cubby, I mommy-daydreamed about having his teacher make house calls during clean-up time.

Every night that week Christian was excited about camp the next day and was heartbroken when it ended. He didn't realize that kindergarten was right around the corner.

KINDERGARTEN

I'm pleased to say that he officially started kindergarten in August of 2016. He made friends with another little boy. They touched each other's faces to "see" what each other looked like. His teacher told me that Christian and the other little boy loved sitting at the same table, although Christian randomly sniffed the little boy's hands.

Yup.

I don't know where he picked it up, but if someone comes up to him and touches him without talking, he will take their hands and sniff. It's the same way with people he's already met, unless the person is extremely familiar.

The child has zero concept of personal space. It's completely embarrassing, but it makes for some fun conversations. People have been so forgiving when it comes to Christian, and it sounded like his new table friend didn't mind either.

Best buds for life.

Lacey Buchanan
December 4, 2015

I have been a mother for almost five years now, and one thing motherhood has taught me is that raising kids is full of highs so high you think it can't get any better, and lows that make you feel like you're scraping the bottom. And sometimes all those highs and lows can come at once.

Since summer camp Christian has made great strides using his cane. The school teaches him to perfect his skills, as well as learn the etiquette involved. Thankfully he isn't using it as a sword yet, so little Chandler is safe for the time being.

One area we are working on is how to hold the cane properly in a crowded area. I'm so afraid Christian will accidentally trip someone, so we work on this skill a lot. He will soon begin orientation and mobility therapy at his new school, which is basically physical therapy for kids with vision impairment. He's progressing well and making friends. I could not be happier with how kindergarten is working out.

Along with the therapy at his school, Christian still attends his normal weekly therapies. However, I'm pleased to announce that Christian has moved on to more advanced skills. He is learning detail-oriented tasks such as sorting items that are "same" or "different."

Another win is that Christian is learning to identify items by touch. For example, if I put a piece of fruit in his hands, he can tell me that it is an apple and describe it as smooth, cool, and that it smells yummy! I look forward to the day when Christian takes a bite of the apple, but we aren't there yet.

Perhaps one of my favorite achievements is that Christian speaks in full sentences most of the time! While still not at an age-appropriate level, his vocabulary is large and growing. To put this in perspective, Chandler is three years old, and both he and Christian speak at a similar age level. This is impressive considering less than a year ago he was only speaking two to three word phrases.

Medically, Christian still needs some surgeries to help repair his palate (there is a small hole that opened since his last repair). Thankfully this procedure isn't considered "major surgery." He also needs lip revision surgery to allow his lips to better move and form words. Once that happens, I'm confident we'll notice an even more dramatic increase in his vocabulary and speech.

Chris and I are extremely proud of Christian. He is truly our superhero.

Harmony at Home

Along with Christian's successes Chris and I have found harmony in our marriage. Counseling has turned out to be extremely helpful. With God's grace we're learning to let go of past hurts. A fresh start doesn't happen overnight, and I'm still frustrated at times, but I have to choose forgiveness so bitterness doesn't creep back in.

Counseling also taught Chris and me that we won't always be able to split our responsibilities fifty-fifty. Marriage isn't a fairy tale, and there isn't always a happily ever after. Instead marriage is a daily sacrifice to put your spouse's needs in front of your own. There are times when Chris and I loved each other but didn't like each other, and those were the times I had to let God dictate my choices instead of my feelings.

God says to show mercy and grace, not throw a temper tantrum, so while we haven't always gotten it right, we've grown tremendously throughout this process.

Honestly, I've seen an amazing change in my husband. He

never misses a photo session or family outing. If Chandler needs a new diaper, he simply changes it because it's what his son needs. He'll fix lunch for the boys if they're hungry and help me around the house. While I was studying for the bar exam, he made himself available to run errands, handle bath times, and tuck kiddos into bed.

A few Sundays ago our pastor met us in the foyer after the service for an update.

"How do you forgive?" he asked me.

I grabbed Chris's hand.

"Minute by minute."

Now we are a team, ready to face each challenge ahead together. While Christian has undergone some of the most extensive surgeries imaginable, we know there are dozens more in his future. Our plan is to continue with the most medically necessary procedures and work our way down. The surgeon we love always gave us options, wanted to know our priorities, and built a plan with us instead of matter-of-factly saying, "This is what we're going to do."

Chris and I have decided that mileage isn't a determining factor when it comes to Christian's care, so there is a possibility that we may travel to New York since that's where Christian's surgeon moved.

FRIENDS AND GOOD FOOD

God has blessed us with an incredible support system. The Internet may be full of spiteful, mean-spirited people, but the Internet is also how I met some of the most incredible women in my life.

Each year a few of the friends I've met online fly in to Tennessee for our annual Food Appreciation Trip, or FAT for short. Sweet Marisa drives down for a long weekend; Sara, mom of two sons slightly older than mine, flies in from Colorado. One year she brought her kiddos, and the four boys couldn't get enough of each other.

Julie from Texas has a precious little boy named Ryan who shares Christian's birthday. He also has special needs, so we find solace in each other's experiences. She couldn't make it to our most recent reunion, so she surprised me by showing up at my law school graduation.

Hailing from Australia is Cassandra, who carves out time in her schedule to stay in the States for a few weeks. She and I met through Facebook and quickly became best friends. We talk every day, and she continuously tries to get me to visit Australia, even though I'm terrified of flying. I'm more than happy to let her do the air travel and provide lodging as long as she wants to stay!

We're an unlikely bunch, brought together by God's design. This trip gives me a few days to be a woman, a friend, Lacey. It also provides an opportunity to be a tourist in my backyard. We've done the Grand Ole Opry tour, visited the Loveless Café, and strolled Broadway. Planning for #FAT2017 has commenced, so I welcome all Nashville foodies to share your favorite haunts.

LAW AND ORDER

I'm thrilled to announce that I graduated from law school and passed my bar exam on the first try! I plan to apprentice for a while and really get experience under my belt before opening my own law practice. I've been to court as a civilian mother fighting for her child, and I look forward to reentering a courtroom as a lawyer fighting for someone else's.

It's my dream to provide counsel for families who are struggling through the red tape of an uncaring system. Four years ago when I couldn't afford the hourly costs of an attorney (let alone the retainer), I vowed to set my rates at a price that wouldn't overwhelm a family already struggling to make ends meet. I look forward to making that dream a reality.

Similarly Chris is excited about starting college and earning his business degree. He loves his insurance job and is eager to grow with the company. Now that I'm out of school, it's his turn to hit the books.

God knows I can't believe how much our life has changed since that hateful Facebook comment. I think back to how heartbroken and nervous I was when I created the video, and I marvel how God transformed the hurt into hope.

I sometimes wonder if Christian's circumstance makes fellow believers take a deeper look at their own faith, their own ideas about who God is. People approach us out of pure curiosity, then are unable to pull themselves away because they want to know more about Christian.

About *Christian*.

Not about his disability.

Christian is so full *joie de vivre*, so full of life that no one can look at him and think his life is anything but sunshine. He breaks down barriers—he negates the assumption that people with a disability have a terrible existence.

Christian is not a mistake.

Our pain has been heavy, and God allowed the darkness to flood in, but in the midst of sorrow there comes peace. Christian simply reflects the light of his Creator.

If God can use Christian's life to perpetuate love and kindness for other precious children, then I'll continue to give my all every day with God's strength.

Seeing our story compiled in black-and-white meant we relived each aspect of the last several years. So thank you, reader, for joining us on this adventure. As I pored through baby books and old photos, I cried with joy as well as heartache. The reminders of

God's overwhelming love renewed my faith, and I pray God uses our journey to touch your life as well.

I'd love to hear how. You can connect with us on Facebook at https://www.facebook.com/LaceyandChristianBuchanan/.

> *If God can use Christian's life to perpetuate love and kindness for other precious children, then I'll continue to give my all every day with God's strength.*

If we're blessed to cross paths one day, be prepared for Christian to run his hands over you inappropriately. His hands are his eyes, and although I constantly tell him not to grab people, he doesn't listen. In typical toddler fashion Christian does what Christian wants.

If you kneel down and speak to him, he'll come toward the sound of your voice. Let him place his hands on your face to learn the curve of your cheeks, feel the shape of your nose, the feel of the bones around your eyes. When he sniffs at you, don't be alarmed—he'll recognize your unique aroma the next time we meet. And if your heart begins to sadden when you look at his sweet face, when you imagine the journey he has ahead, don't worry.

Christian doesn't have to wait to see what life offers.

He has the world at his fingertips.

NOTES

INTRODUCTION

1. Craig D. Lounsbrough, *An Intimate Collision*, as quoted in *"An Intimate Collision* Quotes," GoodReads.com, accessed August 23, 2016, http://www.goodreads.com/work/quotes/43561163-an-intimate-collision-encounters-with-life-and-jesus?page=2.

CHAPTER 1
TRUSTING GOD WHE

1. And here we are today—I graduated from law school in May 2016 and Christian started kindergarten the following August.

CHAPTER 2
TRUSTING GOD WHEN THINGS GO WRONG

1. *The Doctors* staff, "Raising a Child With a Severe Cleft Palate," *The Doctors*, February 26, 2014, accessed August 23, 2016, http://www.thedoctorstv.com/articles/1015-raising-a-child-with-a-severe-cleft-palate.
2. See Romans 8:38–39.
3. See Psalm 139:14.
4. See Romans 8:28.

CHAPTER 3
FOR BETTER OR FOR WORSE

1. Gary Chapman, *The Five Love Languages* (Chicago: Northfield Publishing, 2010).

CHAPTER 4
TESTS, TRIALS, AND TEARS

1. Francine Rivers, *Redeeming Love* (Colorado Springs, CO: Multnomah Books, 2007), 164.

CHAPTER 5
STRENGTH IN WEAKNESS

1. See 2 Corinthians 12:9.

CHAPTER 6
A LONG STRETCH OF NIGHT

1. "Fentanyl Drug Information," accessed August 25, 2016, http://www.narconon.org/drug-information/fentanyl.html.
2. "Methadone," accessed August 25, 2016, https://www.drugs.com/methadone.html.
3. Mike Elvin, "The Ponseti Method for Clubfoot Correction: An Overview for Parents," adapted from a presentation by Dr. John Blanco and Dr. David Scher, posted February 16, 2006, reviewed May 20, 2009, accessed August 25, 2016, https://www.hss.edu/conditions_the-ponseti-method-for-clubfoot-correction.asp.
4. See Romans 8:28.
5. See Jeremiah 29:11.
6. See Isaiah 55:8–9.
7. See Romans 8:38–39.
8. See Luke 22:42.

CHAPTER 9
A COMMUNITY OF SPECIAL KIDS

1. Special Kids Therapy and Nursing Center, Welcome page, accessed August 25, 2016, http://www.specialkidstn.com/#welcome.
2. See Psalm 46:1.

CHAPTER 10
HATRED FROM BEHIND THE KEYBOARD

1. See Matthew 25:40, 45.

2. Natalie Brumfield, "South Korea Pastor's 'Drop Box' Saves Abandoned Babies From Infanticide," LifeNews.com, May 28, 2013, accessed August 30, 2016, http://www.lifenews.com/2013/05/28 /south-korea-pastors-drop-box-saves-abandoned-babies-from -infanticide/.

3. Lee Jong-rak, in *The Drop Box*, documentary by Arbella Studios, trailer viewed at Brumfield, "South Korea Pastor's 'Drop Box' Saves Abandoned Babies From Infanticide."

4. Sarah Terzo, "Pregnant Couples Who Plan to Abort Down Syndrome Babies Defend Their Choice," August 23, 2014, accessed August 25, 2016, http://liveactionnews.org/pregnant-couples-who -plan-to-abort-down-syndrome-babies-defend-their-choice/; Cassy Fiano, "If Down Syndrome Parents Won't Defend Their Right to Life, Then Who Will?," April 3, 2013, accessed August 25, 2016, http://liveactionnews.org/if-down-syndrome-parents-wont-defend -their-right-to-life-then-who-will/.

CHAPTER 11
THE VIRAL VIDEO

1. Susan Donaldson James, "Lizzie Velasquez: 'Ugliest Woman' Video Changed My Life for the Better," *Today*, August 31, 2015, accessed August 26, 2016, http://www.today.com/health/lizzie-velasquez -ugliest-woman-video-changed-my-life-better-t41361; Mike Celizic, "Meet Woman Who Can't Gain Weight: At 21, She's 60 Pounds," *Today*, July 6, 2010, accessed August 26, 2016, http://www.today .com/id/38105383/ns/today-today_health/t/meet-woman-who-cant -gain-weight-shes-pounds.

2. "How Do You Define Yourself?," talk given by Lizzie Velasquez at TED^X, uploaded January 24, 2014, accessed August 26, 2016, http:// tedxtalks.ted.com/video/How-do-you-define-yourself-Lizz; I'm With Lizzie, accessed August 26, 2016, http://imwithlizzie.com/.

CHAPTER 12
GIFTS FROM STRANGERS

1. See Matthew 25:40.

CHAPTER 14
ANOTHER BUCHANAN BABY!

1. Janette Oke, *Love's Long Journey* (Grand Rapids, MI: Bethany House, 2003), 178.

2. See Joel 2:26.

3. Mark Twain: "Boy, n: a noise with dirt on it." See "Wisdom of the Ages," accessed August 26, 2016, http://www.eristic.net/quotes.php.

CONNECT WITH US!

CHARISMA HOUSE

(Spiritual Growth)

 Facebook.com/CharismaHouse

 @CharismaHouse

 Instagram.com/CharismaHouseBooks

SILOAM

(Health)

 Pinterest.com/CharismaHouse

REALMS

(Fiction)

 Facebook.com/RealmsFiction